Indiana Cooks!

Indiana Cooks!

season somewhere, but that doesn't guarantee it will taste its best when it gets off the truck or plane. The best chefs understand and respect the dictates of seasonality.

They also respect the importance of buying locally, from nearby farms and ranchers, and from artisan producers. We in Indiana are blessed to live in the midst of a region that produces glorious vegetables and fruits and grains; superb lamb, venison, duck, poultry, buffalo, and grass-fed beef; and incredible dairy products (including some of the world's best goat cheese from Capriole Farms in Greenville, delicious cheddars from The Swiss Connection in Clay City, and first-rate yogurt and fresh cheeses from Traders Point Creamery in Zionsville, to name just a few). Not only does supporting these local producers help keep the food dollar in the state, where it bolsters the local economy, but these locally produced foods are just plain better tasting and more healthful than mass-produced foods.

Supporting their commitment to finding the best-tasting ingredients, some of the chefs in this book are members of the Slow Food movement, an international response to globalization and fast food that emphasizes eating seasonally, regionally, and convivially—a movement embraced by some of the leading chefs in the world. There are already four local Slow Food groups in Indiana (Michiana, Indy, Bloomington, and Kentuckiana), and more are in the works. It is possible to be a good chef without relying on the principles of Slow Food, but good, fresh, flavorsome ingredients make the job easier.

Good Eating

So, have we discovered all the great places to eat in Indiana? Surely not, even among the fine-dining restaurants we have been focusing on. The task of discovery has been a fun and rewarding one, however, and we will not give it up.

As the restaurant business is notoriously fluid, some of the places in this book may be gone by the time you read this, and other super places will have appeared. This book is only a snapshot of fine dining in Indiana.

We welcome suggestions and comments from readers who may agree or disagree with our choices.

It is worth remembering, though, that every time we spend a dollar on food, we are casting a vote for the kind of world we want to live in. Slow, delicious, seasonal, and creative, versus fast, standardized, corporate, and predictable: the choice is ours.

We wish you all good eating in America's heartland!

Their very success jeopardizes the small, independent restaurants that are not backed by deep pockets. Fine-dining restaurants have higher costs than their corporate cousins (think crystal glasses versus plastic tumblers, china versus crockery, linens versus paper placemats) and many fewer economies of scale. It's not easy for them to compete with the crush of chain-restaurant mass marketing and the overwhelming name recognition it brings, with the lure of the familiar and the predictable.

But independent restaurants can offer things the chains usually do not: imaginative and inventive menus that have not been test-marketed to appeal to the lowest common denominator in taste; ingredients that have been chosen for seasonality and flavor rather than cost efficiency and easy, year-round availability; and service that is individual and courteous rather than overly friendly and gimmicky.

Of course not all independent restaurants meet these standards. But the ones in this book do, and so do many others. Searching them out is its own reward.

Superb Cooking

Finally, the restaurants in this book are also distinguished by the skill of the chefs who cook in them. All the chefs we have chosen have a certain something—a knack, a flair, a sure and instinctive touch with ingredients—that differentiates them from their more pedestrian peers. They are truly good cooks.

Good cooking is hard to define, but it is more than just good knife skills and the ability to tell when a piece of meat is medium-rare. It involves a sixth sense—an ability to know how ingredients will come together to produce something more than the sum of its parts. It is not enough to combine exotic ingredients simply because they are exotic, or to pile flavor upon flavor indiscriminately (producing what one friend calls "too many notes"). Good cooking is a matter of balance and finesse and judgment—of generosity and extravagance, yes, but tempered by restraint and discipline.

Not only are all the chefs in this book good cooks, but almost all are characterized by a commitment to using seasonal ingredients, locally produced where possible, and to patronizing artisan producers who use small-scale methods instead of mass-production techniques that take the craftsmanship out of food preparation.

Seasonality is the key to tasty food. One of the hallmarks of a good chef is the willingness to forgo putting a favored dish on the menu when its ingredients are not in season—to search and wait patiently for the ripest tomatoes, the most perfectly aged cheese, the plumpest duck, the sweetest berries, the tenderest veal, the nuttiest scallops.

Seasonal eating used to be the only possible way to go—what couldn't be preserved when crops were harvested was eaten on the spot at its most delicious moment. Today global trade and rapid transport mean that we live in a world where everything is in

Then we got in the car and drove around the state and ate, and ate, and ate some more.

The restaurants we have chosen are all different, but they have some things clearly in common. They provide a great fine dining experience, they are independently owned, and the chefs have a sure and intuitive sense of how to put a dish together.

The Restaurant Experience

So what is it that makes a great restaurant experience? What are we really looking for when we go out to eat?

Once upon a time, eating out was an occasion, a rare excuse to dress up and splurge, to relax and be waited on, to be treated like minor royalty while enjoying a meal that was not something one could cook at home.

But today, for many of us, eating out has just become a time-saver for overcommitted, exhausted people who have run out of energy by the end of the day. The restaurant industry's share of the food dollar has climbed to 46.4 percent in 2004; the industry claims its sales have gone from $42.8 billion in 1970 to $440.1 billion in 2004. Much of that increase comes from the growth in fast-food and chain restaurants.

When life is busy and hectic, a good restaurant is one that is quick, convenient, and cheap, but that's not dining out in the old-fashioned sense. That kind of dining out goes back to the origins of the word restaurant. As Rebecca Spang tells us in *The Invention of the Restaurant,* before they were ever places to eat, restaurants were things to be eaten. From the French "to restore," they were brothy soups made from meat and frequently very little else, served as restoratives to invalids in pre-Revolutionary France.

Eventually, the establishment where one went to drink a restaurant began to be called a restaurant as well. After the French Revolution, the unemployed chefs of the former aristocracy came to Paris looking for work, and helped to elevate the restaurant to something approximating its present grandeur. The rest is culinary history.

The restaurants we have chosen in this book are all true to the origins of the word. They are restorative places where one is cosseted and fed well, and sent back to the fray of daily life feeling replenished and recharged.

Independent Restaurants

It's hard to preserve the idea of dining out as refuge and respite, however, when chain restaurants rule in America—their electric logos casting a flashy neon glow along our highways and strip malls and shopping centers. Given the busy lives of Americans, it's not difficult to understand why the chains are so popular: their food is affordable, fast, and filling.

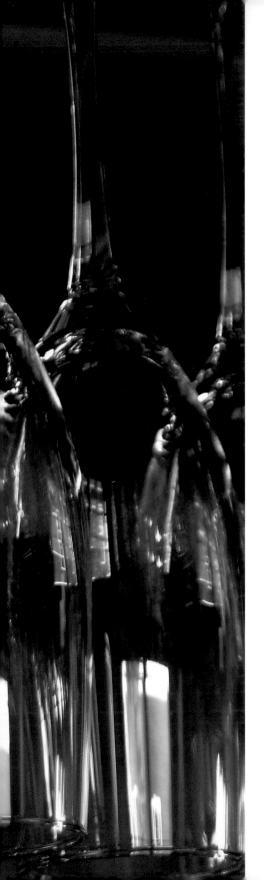

Introduction

Our big-city friends laugh when we say we are writing a cookbook about great Indiana restaurants. From the culinary heights of New York or Los Angeles, they smile tolerantly (or not) at the quaint idea that we in the heartland could produce first-rate dining that might actually warrant a visit.

Let them smirk. Indiana has found its place on the culinary map.

Sure, we have more than our share of chain restaurants and strip-mall fast food. But we also have superb ethnic restaurants, an abundance of good down-home comfort food spots, and a growing and thriving white tablecloth–restaurant scene that rivals the top progressive regional American cooking around the nation.

In the last ten years or so, we have been lucky enough to see an upsurge in places serving well-crafted, creative food made with fresh seasonal—often local—ingredients. It is possible to eat as well in Indianapolis as it is in Chicago, Atlanta, Houston, or Seattle—all cities well known for their lively dining options.

In this book we feature fifteen of the best of those Indiana fine-dining establishments, all of them independently owned. Picking the top restaurants in the state is a challenge, albeit an enjoyable one, and it is ultimately a subjective business. The final list of chefs and restaurants in this book is influenced by the kinds of food we like, no doubt about it. But in an effort to be as inclusive as possible, we scoured local newspapers and regional magazines and talked to food writers, wine sales reps, chefs, and dedicated eaters across Indiana.

Acknowledgments

We are grateful to all the Indiana chefs in this book who took precious time from their busy schedules to adapt their recipes for the home kitchen and write them out (a more painstaking exercise than you might guess), and who then prepared them beautifully so we could get the photographs you see in this book. They are our "food stylists" and we thank them.

We are also grateful to Jerry Wright for devoting a whole summer to trying out new restaurants around Indiana, to Beth Feickert, chief ingredient-chaser and prep cook (and tireless recipe taster), and to Amy Novick, who repeatedly put up with Tom's arriving home after a photo shoot with his appetite spoiled for dinner.

Finally, we thank the folks at Indiana University Press for their support in producing this book: Gayle Sherwood, Linda Oblack, Emmy Ezzell, Sharon Sklar, and Dawn Ollila are among those who helped pull this book together. We thank them for their good work.

reminder that, in the immortal words of Dorothy, of *The Wizard of Oz* fame, "There's no place like home."

With great passion and conviction, *Indiana Cooks!* invites us all to the table, offering exciting new adventures in our own culinary exploits. It bridges our communities the restaurants, the producers, and the people—and brings the movement to each of us in a meaningful way. Christine Barbour and Scott Feickert have assembled recipes from some of the finest chefs in our state—chefs who open our eyes to the bounty of our own local harvests.

Each chapter of the book invites us to experience the passionate force that drives these chefs. We hear their stories, learn what motivates them, and share their experiences through the dishes they help us to create and enjoy. These caretakers of the independent restaurant forgo the large-scale purchasing power and franchise support provided by national chain restaurants for the freedom to create. This freedom allows these chefs to cultivate and promote the use of local ingredients and regional traditions.

Indiana Cooks! is a sincere gift. It is also a tribute to the independent chef's vision and the excellent food that can be created. Most importantly, it is an invitation for us to make the same discovery—and to create a revival in our own kitchens.

DAVID FLETCHER
BLU Culinary Arts
Bloomington, Indiana

Foreword

Every Friday evening for nearly a year, I would finish with my last patient, jump in my car, and make the familiar fifty-two-minute drive north to catch the last flight to New York. By the time I landed and took a taxi to my apartment, it was nearly midnight. After a few hours of sleep, I was up and on my way to school—culinary school. I had decided to head to one of the great food capitals of the world to become a chef.

It was a one-hour walk to school, and each weekend I tried to take a different route. I wanted to learn the city—after all, that was what this entire adventure was about: learning and experiencing.

During those months I learned many things, but what has stayed with me is an awareness of the freshness that surrounds us. Unexpectedly tucked away at the edge of a park, or in a vacant lot, was green market after green market. Staffed by people who had fought their way into the city, the booths were little oases in a sea of concrete. New Yorkers flocked there to get the one thing the city denies them, fresh locally grown produce. I shared their hunger. My eyes opened to the bounty surrounding me, I began to search out restaurants that used local produce, people that believed the pursuit of freshness was worthwhile, and organizations (like Slow Food) that helped to preserve it.

The irony of my weekly pilgrimage to New York eventually became apparent. There I was, driving through the produce-rich Indiana countryside on my way to the concrete jungle, only to find a renewed appreciation of the local bounty that surrounds us all. *Indiana Cooks!* is a necessary

CONTENTS

This book is a publication of

Quarry Books

an imprint of
Indiana University Press
601 North Morton Street
Bloomington, IN 47404-3797 USA

http://iupress.indiana.edu

Telephone orders   800-842-6796
Fax orders   812-855-7931
Orders by e-mail   iuporder@indiana.edu

The paper used in this publication meets the minimum
requirements of American National Standard for
Information Sciences—Permanence of Paper for Printed
Library Materials, ANSI Z39.48-1984.

Printed in China

Library of Congress Cataloging-in-Publication Data

Barbour, Diana Christine, date-
Indiana cooks! : great restaurant recipes for the
home kitchen / Christine Barbour and Scott Feickert ;
photographs by Tom Stio.
p. cm.
ISBN 0-253-34664-9 (cloth : alk. paper)
1. Cookery. 2. Restaurants—Indiana. 3. Cooks—
Indiana. 4. Menus. I. Feickert, Scott. II. Title.
TX714.B365 2005
641.59772—dc22
2005001857

1 2 3 4 5 10 09 08 07 06 05

Great Restaurant Recipes for the Home Kitchen

Christine Barbour and Scott Feickert

Photographs by Tom Stio

Indiana Cooks!

BONGE'S TAVERN
Tony Huelster, Chef/Owner

9830 West 280 North
Perkinsville, Indiana 46011

765-734-1625
www.bongestavern.com

MENU

• **Smoked Salmon Tower**

• **Beer-Braised Beef Brisket with Kohlrabi au Gratin**

• **Harger Duck**

• **Bonge's Fresh Peach Cobbler**

Tony Huelster Bonge's Tavern

THE MORNING WE ARRIVE AT BONGE'S Tavern to chat with Tony Huelster, a mountain of kitchen disasters has piled upon him, beginning with the broken thermostat in his walk-in refrigerator. He is mighty exasperated but laughing, taking another crazy day in the restaurant business in stride.

As he talks about his career and his cooking, Huelster's big frame is relaxed, his expressive face and his deep mellow voice rich with humor and conviction. For all his good nature, the overwhelming impression he radiates is one of solid confidence—in himself, his cooking, his restaurant, and his ability to cope with annoying mishaps.

Bonge's Tavern is a phenomenon in the northern Indianapolis area that has people packing the parking lot and partying out of their cars, waiting

for tables on busy weekend nights. They could get into many another, fancier place without any wait at all, but the Perkinsville pork tenderloin, fresh fish, and comfort-food classics like brisket braised in beer—perhaps with house-smoked salmon to start and sugar cream cake to finish—keep them cooling their heels until a bright plastic-covered table opens up.

One way or another, Huelster has been preparing for this restaurant since he was about ten. His piano teacher mom, "an awesome cook," worked late, and young Tony took to cooking the family meals just so they could eat at a normal hour. From the age of fourteen he worked in restaurants, increasingly interested in the cooking side of the business.

A college major in forestry and wildlife biology took him from Indianapolis, where he had lived since the eighth grade, to Vincennes and on to the University of Montana. Bad job prospects in his chosen field left him thinking, at nineteen, that he should go back to what he knew how to do best, which was cooking.

While he was still in Montana, he found himself in the kitchen of the first "true chef" to come his way, and his experience working with someone with a formal culinary education opened his eyes. He moved back to Indianapolis with the goal of becoming a chef. There he trained with some of the best chefs in town, landing in the kitchens at Meridian Hill Country Club, the Golden Lion in Carmel, and the Glass Chimney, where he ended up staying for thirteen years. In 1993 he took a job running the kitchen at Foxfire's, the Muncie restaurant owned by cartoonist Jim Davis.

When Foxfire's closed in 1999, Huelster had the opportunity to take over Bonge's Tavern. With a cool bar, and the rustic feel of the northern Michigan areas where he loved to fish and hunt, the place was a natural for him and for the kind of food he likes to cook, and he knew he could make it go.

And go it did. Because he had devoted customers in Muncie and Carmel, people came immediately to the little restaurant in rural Perkinsville. By his first summer he was on the cover of *Indianapolis Monthly,* and happy patrons have been partying in the parking lot ever since.

The cooking at Bonge's is focused on fresh ingredients and Indiana products, from the produce Huelster grows in his own garden to regional wild mushrooms and locally canned Red Gold tomatoes, the base for his signature soup. His philosophy is that when you eat out you are supposed to enjoy yourself as much as possible. "I'm running a restaurant, not your life," he says with a grin. "Eat here, splurge, then go home and be on a diet." Before you start that diet, try these recipes—they represent some of the ultimate in Indiana comfort food.

Smoked Salmon Tower

Tony Huelster, Bonge's Tavern (Perkinsville)

SALMON TOWER

8 ounces Capriole goat cheese (chèvre),
   softened (see Sources)
1 tablespoon minced fresh tarragon
1 tablespoon diced red onion
2 teaspoons fresh horseradish
½ teaspoon salt
12 ounces sliced smoked salmon

OIL AND VINEGAR DRESSING

2 tablespoons red wine vinegar
1 teaspoon minced fresh tarragon
pinch salt
pinch finely ground black pepper
¼ cup extra-virgin olive oil

1 pint heirloom or pear tomatoes,
   chopped as needed for garnish

Combine goat cheese, tarragon, onion, horseradish, and salt. Stretch out a 12 × 14–inch piece of plastic wrap. Starting at the top, working across and then down, lay out slices of smoked salmon, each piece slightly overlapping, until plastic wrap is covered. With a pallet knife, spread a very thin layer of goat cheese mixture over salmon, stopping ¼ inch from each edge.

Starting with the bottom edge, use the plastic wrap to lift and fold ½ inch of salmon away from you. Lift wrap off the salmon fold and then roll salmon into log by pulling wrap up and away from you. Rewrap the log in plastic wrap and refrigerate until ready to serve.

Whisk together vinegar, tarragon, salt, and pepper. Slowly whisk in olive oil to incorporate.

To serve, remove plastic wrap from salmon log and cut log into 2-inch slices. Arrange in center of plate and garnish with tomatoes. Sprinkle with oil and vinegar dressing.

Beer-Braised Beef Brisket with Kohlrabi au Gratin

Tony Huelster, Bunge's Tavern (Perkinsville)

BEER-BRAISED BEEF BRISKET

1 beef brisket, about 4 pounds

2 teaspoons salt, plus additional to taste

2 teaspoons black pepper, plus additional to taste

1 teaspoon granulated garlic

1 teaspoon thyme

3 tablespoons Worcestershire sauce

2 medium onions, peeled and sliced

12 ounces beer

8 tablespoons (1 stick) butter

1 cup all-purpose flour

3 ounces ketchup

KOHLRABI AU GRATIN

3 pounds kohlrabi, peeled and sliced

½ cup stemmed and chopped fresh dill

2 teaspoons salt

1 teaspoon white pepper

1½ cups heavy whipping cream

6 ounces breadcrumbs

8 ounces blue cheese, crumbled

8 tablespoons (1 stick) butter, cubed

Preheat oven to 300 degrees. Place brisket in the bottom of a large roaster with lid. Sprinkle with 2 tablespoons salt, 2 tablespoons pepper, garlic, thyme, and Worcestershire sauce. Cover with onions. Add beer around—not on top of—brisket. Cover and bake for 3 to 4 hours until meat is fork tender.

While brisket cooks, make a roux by melting butter in a small, heavy-bottomed saucepan. Whisk in flour and cook until raw flour smell is gone. Set aside.

Remove brisket and cover with foil on cutting board. Strain jus from roaster into a bowl and discard onions and other solids. Skim fat from the top of the jus and pour into medium saucepan. Add ketchup and bring to a boil, slowly whisking in roux until medium thick. Simmer 5 minutes; add salt and pepper to taste. Strain into sauceboat.

Slice brisket very thinly across the grain. Serve with sauce and kohlrabi au gratin.

Preheat oven to 350 degrees. Spray a 9 × 13–inch baking dish with cooking spray and set aside. In a large mixing bowl combine kohlrabi, dill, salt, white pepper, and cream. Toss together and pour into baking dish. In the same bowl combine breadcrumbs and blue cheese, then spread evenly over the top of the mixture in baking dish. Sprinkle evenly with butter. Cover with foil and bake for 1 hour. Let stand 10 minutes before serving.

Harger Duck

Tony Huelster, Bonge's Tavern (Perkinsville)

6 pieces duck breast (7 to 8 ounces each),
   skinned

8 ounces cream cheese, softened

1½ tablespoons diced pickled jalapeños

1 teaspoon salt

1 teaspoon black pepper

12 pieces thick-sliced bacon

thyme, to taste

1½ cups wild rice or wild rice blend, cooked

¾ cup barbecue sauce (Bonge's Tavern
   recommends Big Papa's Bar-B-Que
   Sauce)

Preheat oven to 450 degrees.

Lay duck breast flat on cutting board. Create a pocket by inserting a knife into the middle of one side, pushing knife in almost to the other side, and moving the tip toward each end. Repeat with remaining pieces.

In a small bowl combine cream cheese, jalapeños, salt, and pepper. Using a pastry bag or spoon, stuff duck breasts with cream cheese mixture. Starting at one end of the breast, wrap a slice of bacon around and across breast to seal pocket, overlapping bacon slightly as you wrap. Finish wrapping breast completely with a second slice of bacon. Sprinkle with thyme.

Sauté duck breasts in a hot skillet until bacon is seared, then place in oven. Bake for 10 to 12 minutes. Remove from oven and let rest.

Serve over wild rice and top with barbecue sauce.

Bonge's Fresh Peach Cobbler

Tony Huelster, Bonge's Tavern (Perkinsville)

2½ pounds (approximately 8 to 10) fresh peaches, sliced

2 cups sugar, divided

1 tablespoon ground cinnamon

16 tablespoons (2 sticks) butter, cubed and frozen

1 package spice cake mix

1 cup all-purpose flour

Preheat oven to 350 degrees.

In a large bowl stir together peaches, 1 cup of sugar, and cinnamon. Set aside, stirring from time to time while assembling topping.

In food processor combine spice cake mix, flour, and remaining sugar. (Dry ingredients should fill less than half of the bowl.) Pulse to combine ingredients, then add frozen butter. Pulse to cut butter into dry mixture until particles are between the size of peas and coarse cornmeal. Do not overprocess.

Pour peach base into a 9 × 13 × 2–inch baking dish oiled with cooking spray; level mixture. Spread topping evenly over fruit.

Bake for 30 to 40 minutes, or until topping is brown and crisp. Allow cobbler to cool slightly before serving.

**CITRUS AT THE
CHECKERBERRY INN**
KELLY GRAFF, CHEF
KAREN KENNEDY AND
KELLY GRAFF, PROPRIETORS

*62644 County Road 37
Goshen, Indiana 46528*

574-642-4445
Fax 574-642-0198
www.citrusrestaurant.com

MENU

- **Maryland Lump Crabcakes
  with Tomato-Caper Remoulade**

- **Mushroom Sherry Soup**

- **Wasabi Salmon with Teriyaki-
  Lime Glaze and Green Bean
  Tempura**

- **Chocolate Bourbon Cake with
  Chocolate Ganache**

Kelly Graff

Citrus at the Checkerberry Inn

KELLY GRAFF BECAME A CHEF the way some kids learn to swim—she was tossed in at the deep end. By the time she came up for air she was ready for prime time, cooking as if she'd been born to it.

When Graff and her partner at the Checkerberry, Karen Kennedy, took over the inn from Graff's parents, there was a CIA-trained chef in place, and a menu of four items—rack of lamb, Black Angus beef, Amish chicken, and fish. When that chef decided to leave suddenly, there was no one at the stove. Even though she had never cooked in a commercial kitchen, Graff said, "I'm just going to

have to do it." She was terrified, she says, but her eyes crinkle up and disappear in a self-deprecating grin as she describes it. The trauma does not seem to have been lasting.

Despite—or perhaps because of—her lack of formal training, she cooks in an intuitive way, instinctively knowing what she should do with an ingredient or recipe, even if she can't always describe how she got there. Kennedy says sometimes Graff will create a dish in her sleep, wake up, and say, "Now I know what I want to do with that lamb." Graff also possesses a phenomenal sense of smell—she can detect a missing ingredient in a dish without ever tasting it, and when she builds a recipe, if it doesn't smell right, she starts all over.

Graff has always been interested in food; her mom is an excellent cook, and, having spent part of her childhood on the island of Anguilla, Graff was exposed to all kinds of foods early on. But since taking on the kitchen at Citrus, Graff has developed a passion for cooking. "To me," she says, "it's all about taste and textures." She tries to create dishes so that three or four flavors come into the mouth at the same time, so, for instance, people get a bit of sweet, salty, and hot in one bite. Her wasabi pea–encrusted salmon, a major hit in the restaurant, is a case in point. Graff, a big fan of the fiery little green peas, knew that she wanted to match that nose-stinging horseradish flavor with the salmon, so she thought, why not use the peas themselves for a bit of crunch in the crust? Her innovation makes the mouth sing.

Graff and Kennedy have been working hard at turning Citrus, the Checkerberry's restaurant, into a destination restaurant. The Inn is nestled in the middle of northern Indiana Amish country so picturesque that it is almost a caricature of itself with horses and buggies clip-clopping down the roads, and summer corn reaching high into the sky. The restaurant is a blaze of color; blues, yellows, greens and oranges set the dining room aglow, and sun-drenched paintings by Graff's mother are a vivid reminder of more exotic places.

Theme nights at Citrus (a Spanish wine dinner with tapas, for instance, or the once-a-year Caribbean blowout buffet in March) play up to the brilliant décor, and there is often music (sometimes provided by Kennedy, a professional singer). The mood is friendly, elegant, and generous—much like Graff's cuisine, as you can see in this spicy, sunny menu.

Maryland Lump Crabcakes with Tomato Caper Remoulade

Serves 12 (2 crabcakes per serving)

Kelly Graff, Citrus (Goshen)

TOMATO-CAPER REMOULADE

4 cloves garlic, peeled
2 shallots
1 tablespoon fresh tarragon
2 scallions
1 tablespoon fresh thyme leaves
juice of 1 lemon
2 cups mayonnaise
½ cup capers, drained
1 tablespoon ground cumin
1 tablespoon cayenne pepper
½ cup tomato paste

Place all ingredients in food processor. Puree until just mixed.

CRABCAKES

3 15-ounce cans lump crabmeat
1 large red bell pepper, very finely chopped
1 red onion, very finely chopped
3 stalks celery, very finely chopped
6 scallions, very finely chopped
3 cups mayonnaise
¼ cup chopped parsley
2 tablespoons Old Bay Seasoning
1 egg
1 egg white
2¾ cups panko (Japanese-style breadcrumbs; available in Asian markets), divided
salt and pepper, to taste

clarified butter or olive oil, as needed
lemon wedges, for garnish
fresh greens, for garnish

Pick through crabmeat, discarding shell fragments. To crabmeat add vegetables, mayonnaise, parsley, seasoning, eggs, and ¾ cup breadcrumbs. Mix thoroughly. Season with salt and pepper. Form into 3-ounce patties.

Heat clarified butter or olive oil in a skillet over medium heat. Coat each cake evenly on both sides with remaining breadcrumbs. Cook on both sides until golden brown.

Serve crabcakes with remoulade on the side. Garnish with lemon wedges and fresh greens, if desired.

Mushroom Sherry Soup

Kelly Graff, Citrus (Goshen)

6 large portobello mushrooms, gills and stems removed

olive oil, as needed

8 garlic cloves, minced

4 tablespoons (½ stick) butter

6 yellow onions, cut into 1-inch cubes

2 tablespoons fresh thyme, plus additional for garnish

3 cups good-quality sherry

2 quarts chicken broth

salt and pepper, to taste

2 cups heavy whipping cream

Preheat oven to 350 degrees. Place mushrooms upside down on a large sheet pan. Baste with olive oil and spread minced garlic over them. Roast for 15 to 30 minutes, or until brown.

While mushrooms are roasting, melt butter in a large pot. Over low heat, sweat onions for 20 minutes. Add thyme, sherry, and chicken broth. Chop mushrooms into 1-inch cubes and add to soup. Simmer on low for 30 minutes.

Remove from heat and puree. (Hot soups are most easily pureed with an immersion or hand blender. If pureeing in a countertop blender, cool soup first, then reheat after pureeing.) Season with salt and pepper. Add cream until soup reaches desired consistency. Garnish with thyme.

Wasabi Salmon with Teriyaki-Lime Glaze and Green Bean Tempura

Kelly Graff, Citrus (Goshen)

Teriyaki-Lime Glaze

1 cup water

1 cup sugar

2 cups teriyaki sauce

½ cup soy sauce

1 cup fresh-squeezed lime juice

Wasabi Salmon

6 8-ounce boneless, fresh Norwegian salmon fillets

Vietnamese hot red chili–garlic sauce, as needed (available in Asian markets)

2 cups wasabi peas (available in Asian markets), crushed in food processor

clarified butter, as needed

Green Bean Tempura

1 egg

1 cup flour

¾ teaspoon salt

1 cup beer (light beer makes the crispiest tempura)

1 pound fresh green beans

Teriyaki-Lime Glaze

Bring water and sugar to boil in a medium saucepan. Turn off heat, and add remaining ingredients. Bring to boil for 2 minutes. Remove from heat and set aside.

Wasabi Salmon

Coat each fillet with chili-garlic sauce, then coat with wasabi peas. Heat butter over low heat and sauté fillets on both sides until golden brown; salmon will be medium-rare.

If medium to well-done is desired, roast in 400-degree oven for 5 to 10 more minutes.

Green Bean Tempura

Mix egg, flour, salt, and beer in a bowl; mixture should be thin. Coat beans a few at a time in batter and fry in 375-degree oil until golden brown.

Place finished fillet on plate. Drizzle sauce over fillet and pile tempura on top.

Chocolate Bourbon Cake with Chocolate Ganache

Serves 6

Kelly Graff, Citrus (Goshen)

CHOCOLATE BOURBON CAKE

2 cups all-purpose flour

2 cups sugar

½ cup unsalted butter, softened

¾ cup buttermilk

½ cup water

¼ cup good-quality bourbon

1 teaspoon baking soda

1 teaspoon good-quality vanilla extract

½ teaspoon baking powder

½ teaspoon salt

2 eggs

4 ounces unsweetened baking chocolate, melted and cooled

CHOCOLATE GANACHE

2 pounds bittersweet chocolate, chopped

1 quart heavy whipping cream

vanilla-bean ice cream, optional

fresh berries, optional

CHOCOLATE BOURBON CAKE

Preheat oven to 350 degrees. Spray an angel food or springform pan with nonstick cooking spray. Place all ingredients in a large bowl and beat with electric mixer for 30 seconds. Beat on high for 3 more minutes.

Pour batter into pan and bake 60 minutes, or until toothpick comes out clean. Cool 10 minutes before removing from pan. Cool an additional hour before serving.

CHOCOLATE GANACHE

Scald cream, and pour over chocolate. Stir until smooth.

Serve cake with ganache. Finish with vanilla-bean ice cream and fresh berries, if desired.

Dan Dunville
Dunaway's Palazzo Ossigeno

DUNAWAY'S PALAZZO OSSIGENO
DAN DUNVILLE, CHEF
JEFF DUNAWAY, PROPRIETOR

351 South East Street
Indianapolis, Indiana 46204

317-638-7663
www.dunaways.com

MENU

• **Seared Ahi Tuna with Salsa Cruda**

• **Grilled Vegetable Salad with Balsamic and Port Sauces**

• **Sautéed Halibut with Corn, Morels, and Prosciutto with Corn Broth**

• **Panna Cotta with Fresh Berries**

COOKING IN A BUSY KITCHEN is quite a change from his former life of racing bikes and climbing mountains, but it is what Dan Dunville has always wanted to do.

Fascinated by the whole experience of eating out as a kid, Dunville wanted to go to culinary school from the start, but couldn't convince his parents it would be a good living. So he headed off to Indiana University, majored in bio-anthropology, studied photography, and ended up in the mountains of Nepal and South America, giving guided tours. To get him off the mountaintops, his folks relented, and Dunville went off to the Culinary Institute of America. He hasn't looked back.

Dunville's CIA years were something of a mixed experience, leading him to say that he is "classically trained, but self-taught." He doesn't own to any mentors or singular influences along the way (though he does say he never opens that culinary bible, Thomas Keller's *The French Laundry Cookbook*, without learning something new).

After leaving culinary school, Dunville returned home to Indianapolis, working for Peter George and later doing a two-year stint at the Broad Ripple Steakhouse. Valuable experiences all, but Dunville's heart does not belong to the charcoal grill. In fact, he says he is primarily a fish and sauté guy, adding, "if I never stepped in front of a broiler and grilled a piece of beef, I'd die a happy man."

Fortunately for the reluctant steakhouse chef, in 2004 he won the Indianapolis "Iron Chef" contest. Conjuring up a delectable risotto with the secret ingredient, rhubarb, he caught the attention of Jeff Dunaway, formerly of St. Elmo's and now owner of Dunaway's, in the gorgeous Palazzo Ossigeno building in downtown Indianapolis. There are still steaks on the menu, but here Dunville has greater scope for his culinary talents.

Dunville takes his cooking very seriously, and it shows in the earnest voice and measured manner he uses to talk about it. You could be fooled into thinking that his is an entirely solemn business, until something tickles his sense of humor and he forgets to be reserved. Then his nose crinkles up and his eyes flash with laughter. As he warms to his subject, he laughs more and more frequently, but still, cooking is clearly not a frivolous subject for him.

Dunville built on the foundations he acquired at the CIA to develop a style of cooking that he calls progressive American, with an Asian influence acquired in his travels. When he is cooking he likes to consider flavors and texture, focusing on the whole, stunning creation of a balanced plate. He goes for seasonality and freshness, brooding about the day's features over his morning coffee. It is not until the first plate goes out of the kitchen—the moment when the dish moves from theory to practice—that he relaxes and enjoys the fruits of his creativity.

He says he prefers to cook "little bites" of food, and if you reserve the chef's table in the Dunaway's kitchen you see what he means. Tiny course after tiny course comes to the table, none more than a few mouthfuls, and each exquisite, balanced, and perfect. The menu he creates here offers a full-size version of some of those little bites—all clean, vibrant summer flavors.

Seared Ahi Tuna with Salsa Cruda

Dan Dunville, Dunaway's Palazzo Ossigeno (Indianapolis)

2 tablespoons basil
1 tablespoon cilantro
1 tablespoon mint
1 tablespoon thyme
1 tablespoon chives
1 tablespoon kalamata olives
1 tablespoon garlic
1 tablespoon capers
zest of 1 lemon
juice of 1 lemon
4 tablespoons olive oil, divided
kosher salt and pepper, to taste, divided
1 pound ahi tuna
mixed greens, for garnish

Mince first 8 ingredients separately, then combine. Add lemon zest and lemon juice. Add a portion of olive oil to reach desired consistency. Season with salt and pepper.

Heat remaining olive oil in a large sauté pan over high heat. Season tuna with salt and sear for 10 seconds on each side.

Thinly slice tuna and arrange in a star or shingle on plate. Add salsa around the tuna and garnish with mixed greens.

Grilled Vegetable Salad with Balsamic and Port Sauces

Serves 4

Dan Dunville, Dunaway's Palazzo Ossigeno (Indianapolis)

BALSAMIC SAUCE
2 cups balsamic vinegar
2 tablespoons sugar

PORT SAUCE
½ bottle (1½ cups) tawny port
1 vanilla bean

GRILLED VEGETABLES
1 zucchini, sliced diagonally
1 squash, sliced diagonally
1 red onion, peeled and quartered
1 red pepper, deribbed, seeded, and quartered
2 tablespoons chopped rosemary
2 tablespoons chopped oregano
1 tablespoon chopped thyme
¼ cup olive oil
½ cup balsamic vinegar

6 ounces mixed spring greens
olive oil, to taste

BALSAMIC SAUCE
  Combine balsamic vinegar and sugar. Bring to a boil, then simmer until syrupy and reduced by approximately three-fourths. Set aside.

PORT SAUCE
  Combine port and vanilla bean in a small saucepan. Bring to a boil, then reduce heat and simmer until syrupy and reduced by approximately two-thirds. Remove vanilla bean; set aside.

GRILLED VEGETABLES
  Combine vegetables with herbs, oil, and vinegar in a large bowl and marinate for 30 minutes. Remove vegetables from marinade. Light grill and bring to medium-high heat. Grill vegetables until done, then refrigerate. When vegetables are chilled, cut into small dice, discarding soft, seedy inner portions of zucchini and squash.

  Dress greens with olive oil and center a portion on each salad plate. Top with grilled vegetables, followed by port and balsamic reductions.

Sautéed Halibut with Corn, Morels, and Prosciutto with Corn Broth

Dan Dunville, Dunaway's Palazzo Ossigeno (Indianapolis)

4 ears bicolor corn

2 tablespoons blended oil, plus additional as needed for sautéing halibut

½ yellow onion, diced small

1½ ounces prosciutto, sliced thin

6 ounces morel mushrooms

4 ounces green beans, cut into 1-inch lengths and blanched

2 pounds halibut

salt and pepper, as needed

Wondra flour, as needed for dusting

Cut corn kernels from the cobs and reserve. Place cobs in a pot with enough water to cover; boil for 30 minutes. Strain and reserve broth.

Preheat oven to 400 degrees. Heat 2 tablespoons oil in a large pan over medium heat. Add onion and prosciutto and sauté until onion is translucent. Add reserved corn and sauté 30 seconds. Add mushrooms and green beans and sauté until mushrooms are tender. Deglaze pan with approximately 1½ cups corn broth.

Season halibut with salt and pepper and dust with flour. Sauté in a small amount of oil over medium-high heat until golden brown. Flip and place in oven until done; flesh will be opaque but still tender.

Arrange corn sauté in center of plate and place fish on top. Plate should be brothy but not soupy.

Panna Cotta with Fresh Berries

Dan Dunville, Dunaway's Palazzo Ossigeno (Indianapolis)

1 (¼-ounce) package unflavored gelatin

½ cup water

3 cups heavy whipping cream

½ cup sugar

1 tablespoon vanilla extract

1 cup buttermilk

fresh strawberries, raspberries, and/or blueberries, sliced, for garnish

Spray 6 disposable, 9-ounce plastic cups with cooking spray.

Bloom gelatin by sprinkling it over water and letting it sit for 10 minutes. Do not stir.

Heat cream, sugar, and vanilla in medium saucepan to dissolve sugar. Add gelatin and water to cream mixture and bring to a boil.

Remove from heat and add mixture to buttermilk, being sure not to boil buttermilk. Pour 6 ounces of mixture into each cup. Refrigerate until set.

To serve, invert cup onto plate and puncture bottom with small knife to release panna cotta. Garnish with fresh berries.

Greg Hardesty
Elements

ELEMENTS
GREG HARDESTY, CHEF/OWNER
MICHAEL SYLVIA, GENERAL
MANAGER/OWNER

415 North Alabama Street
Indianapolis, Indiana 46204

317-634-8888

MENU
- **Salad of Baby Beets, Capriole Goat Cheese, Fennel, and Hazelnuts**

- **Roasted Salmon with Its Own Brandade, Indiana Sweet Corn, and Applewood-Smoked Bacon**

- **Lamb Chop with Pearl Barley Risotto and Wild Mushroom Sauce**

- **Warm Peach Tart with Cinnamon Ice Cream and Shagbark Hickory Syrup**

CHEF AND FAMILY MAN, Greg Hardesty constantly attempts to balance the two most important roles in his life. He is, on the one hand, chef and co-owner of one of Indianapolis's hottest restaurants, and on the other hand, a man who took two years off from cooking in San Francisco to stay home with his daughter (whom he credits with saving him from becoming the chef he didn't want to be). Another child later, he is comfortable with the chef he is today and he has the balancing act down—closing his fifty-seat restaurant on Sundays and Mondays to spend time with his family, and creating superb meals for an appreciative clientele the rest of the week.

Hardesty is a solid, soft-spoken man, whose voice gradually warms with passion as he talks

about food and the challenges involved in presenting the highest-quality ingredients in the simplest, most delicious way possible. The cooking at Elements is, well, elemental—everything is natural and made from scratch and ingredients are local where possible. Showing the Japanese and French influences in his training, everything is manipulated as little as Hardesty can manage, and nothing goes on the plate that is not meant to be eaten. No froufrou garnishes or unwieldy herb branches here; Hardesty is a food purist and minimalist at heart.

Working with food was not Hardesty's first career choice. Graduating from Indiana University with a degree in public affairs, he tried selling vinyl siding and insurance, only to reach the firm conviction that he wasn't a salesperson. He had enjoyed working in a restaurant in his Bloomington days, so he went to work at the Glass Chimney in Indianapolis, learning classic Continental food preparation. Newly married, and ready for a change, he moved to Los Angeles and began work in the restaurant empire of Joachim Splichal. There he learned the ethic of California freshness cuisine overlaid with a Mediterranean influence, and picked up a fondness for cooking with olive oil (not, he says with a smile, that there isn't a time and a place for using lots of butter as well).

From L.A. he went to San Francisco, where he worked at Rubicon, learning more about the California/French style of cooking he wanted to do—heavy on seafood, lots of vegetables, everything on the plate having a purpose. Working with a master sommelier he also learned the value of food and wine and getting the pairing right.

It was during his sabbatical at home with his baby daughter in San Francisco that Hardesty and Michael Sylvia, an old friend, began e-mailing back and forth about something they thought was a joke—their plans to open their own restaurant. He's not sure when it became real, but having moved his family back to Indianapolis, he found himself planning to open a sushi restaurant, a cuisine he loved and had long obsessed over.

H_2O Sushi quickly became a hit, but eventually Hardesty found himself adding non-sushi items as specials, and facing a personal challenge—could he go back to the kind of restaurant cooking he had abandoned for the call of family life?

Apparently he could. Within a year of opening Elements with his partner, he was winning accolades and filling the house. Today, he says, "I'm living a dream, I really am." His constantly changing menu reflects the seasons and the bounty of homegrown Indiana food. Elements's fifty seat size lets him direct his food to discerning palates and stay true to his culinary principles. Menus like the one he offers here leave no doubt that they are principles well worth preserving.

Salad of Baby Beets, Capriole Goat Cheese, Fennel, and Hazelnuts

Greg Hardesty, Elements (Indianapolis)

VINAIGRETTE

3 tablespoons rice wine vinegar or champagne vinegar

1 teaspoon Dijon mustard

pinch of salt

¼ cup hazelnut oil

¼ cup extra-virgin olive oil

SALAD

1 cup balsamic vinegar

1 tablespoon sugar

12 baby red beets, boiled in salted water until just cooked through, peeled, and cut into ¼-inch slices

salt and pepper, to taste

6 ounces Capriole goat cheese, softened at room temperature (see Sources)

1 large fennel bulb, sliced paper-thin on mandoline or with sharp knife

1 large shallot, finely chopped

8 leaves basil, sliced into thin strips

¼ cup whole hazelnuts, toasted and coarsely chopped

1 bunch red oak leaf lettuce, stemmed

3 tablespoons extra-virgin olive oil

hazelnuts, for garnish

VINAIGRETTE

Place vinegar, mustard, and salt in bowl. Whisk in oils until emulsified. Set aside.

SALAD

Bring balsamic vinegar and sugar to a simmer in a small saucepan and reduce to ¼ cup. Set aside. Rewhisk vinaigrette. Toss beets with salt, pepper, and just enough vinaigrette to coat lightly. Divide among 4 plates. Divide goat cheese into 4 portions and place a small disk on each beet. Toss fennel, shallot, basil, hazelnuts, salt, and pepper with just enough vinaigrette to coat lightly. Divide fennel mixture into 4 portions and place on top of goat cheese. Finally, toss lettuce with salt, pepper, and just enough vinaigrette to coat lightly, divide into 4 portions, and place on top of fennel mixture. Drizzle balsamic vinegar reduction and olive oil around salad and garnish with a few hazelnuts. (You may not need all the vinaigrette, but it will keep in the refrigerator, covered, for up to a week.)

Roasted Salmon with Its Own Brandade, Indiana Sweet Corn, and Applewood-Smoked Bacon

Serves 4

Greg Hardesty, Elements (Indianapolis)

4 5–6 ounce salmon fillets, skin and pin bones removed, and trimmings reserved

2 ears sweet corn

2 thick slices applewood-smoked (or other good-quality) bacon, cut into ¼-inch dice

BRANDADE

salmon trimmings, reserved from fillet

3 medium Idaho potatoes, cut into ½-inch pieces

3 tablespoons extra-virgin olive oil

1 garlic clove, minced

½ cup heavy whipping cream, warmed slightly in a microwave

salt and pepper, to taste

ONION JUS

3 tablespoons olive oil

2 large red onions, thinly sliced

6 sprigs fresh thyme

2 cups chicken stock

salt and pepper, to taste

2 scallions (green part only), thinly sliced

2 tablespoons unsalted butter

BRANDADE

Roast reserved trimmings in 300-degree oven until just cooked through; set aside. Place potatoes in a medium saucepan, cover with lightly salted water, and bring to a boil. Reduce to simmer and cook until potatoes are tender. Drain potatoes in colander. Lightly warm olive oil and garlic in the same saucepan until garlic just begins to get color, being careful not to burn it. Add potatoes and cream, and season with salt and pepper. Follow your favorite procedure for mashing potatoes. Once potatoes are smooth, add roasted salmon trimmings. Stir lightly to combine, and set aside, keeping warm.

ONION JUS

Warm olive oil in a large sauté pan over medium heat. Add onions and cook until caramelized and deep amber in color. Add thyme and chicken stock and cook until reduced by half. Strain sauce through a fine sieve and set aside.

Cook corn in plenty of lightly salted boiling water until just cooked. Remove to an ice bath until cool. Carefully slice kernels off cobs and set aside. Cook bacon in a large pan over medium heat until crisp, and drain on paper towels. Set aside.

Preheat oven to 300 degrees. Salt and pepper salmon fillets and place in a roasting pan. Cook until just cooked through; salmon should look opaque. While salmon is cooking, gently reheat brandade over low heat. Bring onion jus to boil, and add corn, bacon, and scallions. When hot, add butter 1 tablespoon at a time, and swirl into sauce. Adjust seasoning. When salmon is cooked, place one-fourth of the brandade in center of each plate. Spoon sauce around brandade and place salmon fillet on top.

Lamb Chop with Pearl Barley Risotto and Wild Mushroom Sauce

Greg Hardesty, Elements (Indianapolis)

PEARL BARLEY RISOTTO

4 tablespoons butter

1 onion, cut into ¼-inch dice

1 cup pearl barley

4 cups chicken or vegetable stock

½ cup grated parmesan cheese

2 tablespoons fresh thyme leaves

1 tablespoon chopped fresh flat-leaf parsley

salt and pepper, to taste

MUSHROOM SAUCE

3 tablespoons olive oil

1 pound button mushrooms, sliced

2 cloves garlic, sliced

1 small onion, chopped

2 Roma tomatoes, chopped

2 cups red wine

1 quart chicken stock (or substitute veal stock)

1 cup wild mushrooms (e.g., oyster, shiitake, portobello, chanterelle, cremini), cut in ¼-inch slices

2 tablespoons olive oil

2 tablespoons butter

salt and pepper, to taste

1 (8-bone) rack of lamb

salt and pepper, to taste

2 tablespoons olive oil

2 tablespoons butter

PEARL BARLEY RISOTTO

Warm butter in a large sauté pan over medium heat. Add onions and cook until soft. Add barley and stir to coat with butter. Add 1 cup of stock and stir frequently until almost dry. Repeat with remaining stock, 1 cup at a time, until risotto is completely cooked. (It may not be necessary to use all of the stock.) Remove risotto from heat and stir in cheese, thyme, and parsley. Season with salt and pepper. Set aside and keep warm.

MUSHROOM SAUCE

Warm olive oil in a medium saucepan over medium heat. Add button mushrooms and sauté until golden brown and dry. Add garlic, onion, and tomatoes. Continue cooking over medium heat until vegetables begin to caramelize. Deglaze pan with red wine and reduce until almost dry. Add stock and reduce to 1 cup, skimming as necessary. (It is helpful to strain mushrooms and vegetables out of the sauce about halfway through the reduction process.) While sauce is reducing, sauté wild mushrooms in olive oil and butter in a large pan over medium heat until golden brown. Season with salt and pepper. Stir wild mushrooms into the reduced, strained sauce and set aside.

Preheat oven to 400 degrees. Season lamb with salt and pepper. Warm oil in a large ovenproof sauté pan over medium-high heat and sear lamb on all sides. Place in oven and roast for 12 to 16 minutes, or until medium-rare. Remove lamb from oven and place on a plate to rest for 5 minutes.

Meanwhile, divide risotto among 4 plates. Rewarm mushroom sauce and swirl in butter 1 tablespoon at a time. Spoon sauce around risotto. Slice lamb into 8 single-bone chops and place 2 chops on each plate.

Warm Peach Tart with Cinnamon Ice Cream and Shagbark Hickory Syrup

Serves 4

Greg Hardesty, Elements (Indianapolis)

CINNAMON ICE CREAM
2 cups heavy whipping cream
2 cups whole milk
1 vanilla bean
1 teaspoon cinnamon
1 cup sugar
8 egg yolks

PASTRY
1¼ cups flour
2 tablespoons sugar
¼ teaspoon salt

10⅔ tablespoons (1⅓ sticks) butter, chopped
1 egg yolk
3 tablespoons ice water

FILLING
3 tablespoons butter
4 to 6 peaches, peeled, pitted, and sliced
3 tablespoons sugar

¼ cup shagbark hickory syrup (see Sources)
¼ cup ice cream base, unfrozen, reserved from above
¼ cup pecans, toasted

CINNAMON ICE CREAM

Combine cream and milk in a medium saucepan. Split vanilla bean in half and scrape seeds into saucepan. Add vanilla pod and cinnamon, and simmer. Meanwhile, whisk together sugar and egg yolks in a large bowl until smooth. Slowly pour hot cream mixture into eggs and whisk quickly. Return mixture to saucepan and cook over low heat until thickened. Be careful not to let the mixture boil, or the eggs will curdle. Strain the mixture through a fine sieve and cool completely. Set aside ¼ cup of the ice cream base for garnish. Freeze remaining mixture in ice cream machine according to manufacturer's instructions and keep frozen until ready to use.

PASTRY

Place first 4 ingredients in a mixing bowl. Using paddle attachment, mix on low speed until mixture looks coarse. Add egg yolk and water and continue to mix on low until it just comes together. Turn out onto a floured board and form into a ball. Wrap in plastic and refrigerate for 30 minutes.

Remove dough from plastic wrap and roll out on a floured surface to ⅛-inch thickness. Cut dough into 4 6-inch circles. Place each circle inside a 4-inch tart pan. Allow dough to sink down into bottoms of tart pans and cut off excess dough around tops. Poke bottoms of tart shells several times with a fork and place in refrigerator for 30 minutes.

Preheat oven to 375 degrees. Place chilled tart shells on a baking pan in center of the oven and bake for 8 to 12 minutes, or until shells are light golden brown. Remove from oven and let cool completely. Remove shells from pans.

FILLING

Melt butter in a large sauté pan over medium heat. Add peaches and sugar and cook until warmed through but still holding their shape.

Spoon peaches into pre-baked tart shells and place in middle of large plate. Drizzle syrup and reserved ice cream base around tarts. Top peaches with cinnamon ice cream, sprinkle with pecans, and serve.

Lisa Williams
Joseph Decuis

JOSEPH DECUIS

LISA WILLIAMS, EXECUTIVE
CHEF

ALICE K. ESHELMAN,
PROPRIETOR

191 North Main Street
Roanoke, Indiana 46783

260-672-1715
www.josephdecuis.com

MENU

• Chilled Avocado Soup with
Mango, Lobster, and Lime Salsa

• Salade d'Automne

• Tuna Tartare with Tamari-Ginger
Vinaigrette and Sesame Tuiles

• Wasabi-Miso Kobe Short Rib

LISA WILLIAMS IS FULL OF VERVE AND
vitality, with a strong, mobile face and sparkling
eyes, a gravelly voice and a deep chuckle that
comes rolling up from her toes. She brings the
same zest and passion to conversations about
food that she brings to her cooking, and talking
to her is just plain fun.

Food has been a central part of Williams's
life as long as she can remember. Her Italian
grandparents recreated their native Puglia in
their new home in Ohio, growing imported fig
trees in their immaculate garden and making
wine in the basement, spreading pasta out on
the counter to dry, and filling the house with the
smells of frying eggplant and simmering meat

sauce. For Lisa, these childhood memories are so closely intertwined with the act of eating that even today she will take a bite of something and be struck by the realization that only her sister would be able to taste that food in the exact same way.

Because she was so hooked on food, Williams had long played with the idea of going to culinary school, but instead ended up studying art history and French at Indiana University. Her studies took her to France, where she went to cooking school after all, and then on to Italy. She eventually got a job cooking for a family, and ended up spending two years there.

Back home in Fort Wayne she opened a small lunch place, and tried her hand at a specialty foods store, before becoming a corporate chef. After Williams had cooked for his clients privately for several years, her boss decided to open a restaurant, Joseph Decuis, named after an ancestor. Williams has been the executive chef there ever since (her husband, Chuck Kaiser, is the chef de cuisine).

Being part of a two-chef family means that everyone at home is slightly obsessive about food. Vacations are built around what and where they want to eat, and recipe creation goes on round the clock. Williams will wake up in the middle of the night thinking about food, or a beautiful ingredient that has come into season, or a dish she wants to make. There are lists of menu ideas lying all over the house and lots of food talk, all the time. Williams and Kaiser realized how far gone they were when their daughter Isabella was four. Kaiser asked her one morning what she wanted for breakfast. "I'll have toast and juice," announced the budding foodie, "and then I want to see the menu."

Williams's cooking style has changed dramatically in the nearly twenty-five years she has been at it. At first, she says, she wanted everything—believing that more is better. But now she looks for purer flavors. She says it's more difficult to just let simple things taste good, to let the pure, clean flavors "sing and shine." It's harder to know when to stop than to just keep on going, harder to watch something just sit there. Today, when she sees a gorgeous piece of tuna, she resists the urge to get fussy with it and just wants to eat it raw, maybe with a little bit of oil.

Those pure flavors come from keeping her food seasonal and local whenever possible, "doing the best with the things that are indigenous to where you live." Not only does Joseph Decuis have its own garden, but Williams also supports other regional producers—of cheese, mushrooms, and other good fresh produce. Her food celebrates her own Italian roots and her husband's Japanese heritage, all against the background of her classical French training. This light, bright autumn menu brings it all together.

[37]

Chilled Avocado Soup with Mango, Lobster, and Lime Salsa

Lisa Williams, Joseph Decuis (Roanoke)

SALSA

cooked lobster, diced finely, to taste
mango, diced finely, to taste
tomato, diced finely, to taste
jalapeños, diced finely, to taste
salt and pepper, to taste
freshly squeezed lime juice, to taste

SOUP

4 tablespoons unsalted butter
1 large onion, peeled and finely minced
2 large cloves garlic, peeled and finely minced
1 to 2 teaspoons finely minced jalapeño peppers
2 tablespoons all-purpose flour
5 cups chicken stock (golden, not roasted)
2 medium avocados, peeled, pitted, and diced
juice of ½ lime
sour cream, as needed (up to ⅓ cup)
salt and freshly ground white pepper, to taste

tiny cilantro leaves, for garnish
lime oil, for garnish
chives, for garnish

SALSA

Combine lobster, mango, tomato, and jalapeños in a medium bowl. Season with salt and pepper and add lime juice. Set aside.

SOUP

Melt butter over medium heat in a heavy 4-quart casserole. Add onion, garlic, and jalapeños and cook until soft but not brown. Add flour and cook for 1 minute, stirring constantly. Add chicken stock all at once and whisk until it comes to a boil. Reduce heat, partially cover, and simmer 15 minutes, or until onion and pepper are very tender. Remove from heat and cool.

Puree with an immersion or hand blender or in a countertop blender. Add avocados and lime juice. Puree again. Slowly add sour cream until desired consistency is reached.

Serve soup chilled in martini glasses, garnished with a dollop of salsa, a few tiny cilantro leaves, and a chive as a "straw garnish."

Salade d'Automne

Lisa Williams, Joseph Decuis (Roanoke)

SALAD

1 bunch baby golden beets, cleaned and quartered

6 cups frisée, radicchio, or other seasonal lettuce, cleaned and chilled

1 Asian pear

BANYULS VINAIGRETTE

oil, as needed for sautéing

2 shallots, finely diced

1 tablespoon brown sugar

⅓ cup Banyuls vinegar (or other high-quality sherry vinegar)

1 to 1¼ cups walnut or hazelnut oil

salt and pepper, to taste

PISTACHIO-CRUSTED GOAT CHEESE CROUTON

1½ cups pistachios, shelled

6-inch log of goat cheese

flour, as needed

egg white, lightly beaten

VINAIGRETTE

Sauté shallots in a little oil until transparent. Add brown sugar, letting it melt over shallots. In a blender or food processor, add shallot mix and vinegar and slowly drizzle in oil until emulsified. Season with salt and pepper.

CROUTON

Toast pistachios in a 425-degree oven, watching carefully to make sure they don't burn. When cooled, finely chop. Cut goat cheese from logs into 1-inch disks. Roll disks in flour, dip in egg white, and roll in chopped pistachios until all sides are covered. Set aside.

SALAD

Preheat oven to 425 degrees. Roast beets until fork tender. Let cool, remove skins, and set aside.

Divide greens among salad plates and drizzle or toss with vinaigrette. Just before serving, thinly slice pears and place on greens along with beets. Heat croutons in microwave, about 15 seconds for a single crouton. Increase time if heating all croutons at once, but watch them carefully. Croutons should be very warm, but not running. Place a crouton atop each salad and serve.

Tuna Tartare with Tamari-Ginger Vinaigrette and Sesame Tuiles

Serves 4

Lisa Williams, Joseph Decuis (Roanoke)

Vinaigrette

2 tablespoons fresh lemon juice

1½ teaspoons rice wine vinegar

1 tablespoon tamari

1 teaspoon sambal oelek chili paste
   (available in Asian markets)

½ teaspoon grated fresh ginger

½ teaspoon grated fresh garlic

Tuna Tartare

6 ounces #1 (sashimi) grade ahi tuna, sliced
   and cut into ⅛-inch dice

3 tablespoons tomato, sliced and cut into
   ⅛-inch dice

1 teaspoon purple onion, sliced and cut
   into ⅛-inch dice

2 teaspoons minced chives

Sesame Tuiles

2 tablespoons sesame seeds

¼ teaspoon sugar

pinch of salt

pinch of cayenne pepper

1 egg white

2 teaspoons cornstarch

4 wonton wrappers

vegetable oil, as needed, for frying

1 cup daikon sprouts or micro herbs, for garnish

tobiko (flying fish roe), optional, for garnish

chive oil, optional, for garnish

hot chile oil, optional, for garnish

ginger oil, optional, for garnish

tamari reduction, optional, for garnish

wakame (seaweed) salad, optional, for garnish

Vinaigrette

Whisk together all ingredients until well combined. Set aside.

Tuna Tartare

Combine all ingredients in medium bowl and toss lightly with vinaigrette.

Sesame Tuiles

Combine sesame seeds, sugar, salt, and cayenne pepper and place on plate. In a small bowl whisk together egg white and cornstarch. Paint egg-white mixture on one side of each wonton wrapper. Press into sesame-spice mixture. Heat 1 inch of oil in heavy pot. Deep-fry wontons until brown. Transfer to paper towel to drain.

Serve tuna with tuiles and topped with daikon sprouts or micro herbs. Garnish with tobiko, oils, tamari reduction, and wakame salad, as desired.

Wasabi-Miso Kobe Short Rib

Serves 4 to 6

Lisa Williams, Joseph Decuis (Roanoke)

Marinade

4 cloves garlic, finely chopped

2-inch piece fresh ginger root, peeled and grated

2 jalapeño peppers, finely chopped

4 scallions (white part) chopped, green tops also chopped and reserved

½ cup cream sherry

½ cup mirin (sweet rice wine; available in Asian markets)

juice of 2 limes

¼ cup wasabi

¼ cup Thai garlic-chili sauce (available in Asian markets)

1 cup tamari or low-salt soy sauce (available in Asian markets)

¼ cup miso (fermented soybean paste; available in Asian markets)

3 tablespoons cream sherry

¼ cup honey

2 tablespoons mint

2 tablespoons cilantro

2 tablespoons basil

¼ cup sesame oil

2 tablespoons olive oil

1 (2 to 3 pound) boneless Kobe beef short rib

sticky rice, stir-fried vegetables, or wok-flashed mixed vegetables

spicy mustard, optional, for garnish

red beet oil, optional, for garnish

Marinade

Mix first 6 ingredients (garlic through mirin) in a small saucepan and bring to simmer. Cook approximately 5 minutes. Remove from heat and cool.

In blender combine next 7 ingredients (lime juice through honey) and blend. Add cooled, cooked mixture and blend again. Add reserved scallion greens, herbs, sesame oil, and olive oil and blend until smooth. Chill marinade.

Trim all fat from both sides of rib, then marinate in prepared marinade for at least 2 hours.

Grill on very hot charcoal grill for 3 minutes on each side, turning twice to prevent burning. Grill for total of 6 minutes for rare to medium-rare. Let rest 5 minutes.

Slice in strips across grain of meat as you would London Broil. Serve atop sticky rice, stir-fried vegetables, or wok-flashed vegetables. Garnish completed dish with spicy mustard and red beet oil, if desired.

Thomas Sheridan
LaSalle Grill

LASALLE GRILL

Thomas Sheridan, Chef de Cuisine

Lisa Sheridan, Pastry Chef

Mark McDonnell, Proprietor

115 West Colfax Avenue
South Bend, Indiana 46601

574-288-1155
800-382-9323
www.lasallegrill.com

MENU

• Salad of Beef Carpaccio and Baby Spinach with Grated Italian Gorgonzola and Shallot-Tomato Vinaigrette

• Lobster Pot Pie

• Dijon- and Brown Sugar–Marinated Pork Tenderloin with Creamy Polenta and Andouille Sausage–Pear Compote

• Apple Fritters with Caramel Sauce

FOR TOM SHERIDAN, IT'S ALL ABOUT "creativity under fire," turning out great food for lots of people when you are really busy and the adrenalin is running high. He relishes the fast pace and electric energy that the kitchen generates on a hectic night, and he is thrilled when people love the food he turns out.

Sheridan should know all about it—he grew up in the restaurant business. His parents had a family restaurant where he worked from the time he was small, and he never really considered doing anything else with his life. He always knew he would be a chef, and he still thinks it's a great job.

Every day is different—hard and demanding, but also fun. He likes the challenge of balancing

practical financial and creative culinary considerations; "you have to stay in business and keep your fire lit," he says. And he also likes the fact that sometimes, just making it through a hard night "feels like a win."

Sheridan got his training working in restaurants (where he says he was fortunate to learn from some great chefs), earning a culinary degree from Vincennes University, and attending short regional cooking courses at the Culinary Institute of America. He came to the LaSalle Grill in 1991, left for a while, and came back again to serve as sous chef for two years. He has been the restaurant's chef de cuisine ever since.

Sheridan loves the wide range of opportunities the restaurant gives him to practice his craft. The LaSalle Grill is a contemporary American steakhouse that is "more than a steakhouse." Sheridan can turn out an expertly grilled filet mignon topped with "Tabasco onions" (a house favorite), but he also changes the menu daily to reflect the seasons, the fresh fish that is available, and even a few dishes (like risottos, gnocchi, and polenta) that evoke his Italian heritage on his Mom's side.

He can also produce a degustation of at least seven courses, cater an outdoor meal for four hundred through LaSalle's Grill 2 Go customized catering program, cook with guest chefs for charitable events, put on wine dinners, or entertain parties in a private dining room. The variety keeps the job fun and just stressful enough to be interesting—ensuring that that adrenalin high is never too far away.

In designing his dishes, Sheridan loves to work with taste, color and "the crunch factor." He especially likes playing with the smoky flavor given off by their hardwood grill—balancing the robust woodsiness with a sweet balsamic or honey glaze. The restaurant is committed to serving fresh seasonal food, patronizing local producers where possible, but going wherever is necessary to find the finest.

There is an open friendliness in Sheridan's face that makes him look younger than his thirty-three years, in spite of a goatee and a baseball cap that shades his dark eyes as he talks. He is old enough to be a father of three small kids, however. Their mom, pastry chef Lisa Sheridan, is responsible for the restaurant's desserts, including their luscious, signature crème brûlée flavored with Grand Marnier and vanilla.

The LaSalle Grill's changing show of local art on the walls, gorgeous fresh flowers on the tables, and emphasis on superb service all complement the delicious food, ensuring that it is not only on Notre Dame football weekends that the place is full. If you can't get a reservation, try cooking this delicious fall/winter menu for yourself.

Salad of Beef Carpaccio and Baby Spinach with Grated Italian Gorgonzola and Shallot-Tomato Vinaigrette

Serves 4

Tom Sheridan, LaSalle Grill (South Bend)

8 ounces beef tenderloin, frozen to aid slicing

1 cup heirloom tomatoes, cut into ⅛-inch dice

2 shallots, cut into ⅛-inch dice

1 tablespoon honey

1 tablespoon coarse-ground mustard

½ cup sherry vinegar

1 cup extra-virgin olive oil

10 ounces baby spinach, washed and spun dry

gorgonzola cheese, frozen, to taste

freshly ground black pepper, to taste

Thinly slice beef. Arranges slices on parchment paper and refrigerate.

To make vinaigrette, combine tomatoes, shallots, honey, mustard, and vinegar. Whisk in olive oil until emulsified.

Toss spinach in just enough vinaigrette to coat each leaf. Portion dressed greens among 4 salad plates. Top with sliced beef, and finish by grating gorgonzola over salad using thinnest grater available. Top with black pepper.

Lobster Pot Pie

Tom Sheridan, LaSalle Grill (South Bend)

CRUST

16 tablespoons (2 sticks) unsalted butter

2 cups all-purpose flour

½ teaspoon paprika

¼ teaspoon salt

¼ teaspoon baking powder

½ cup yogurt

ice water, as needed

FILLING

butter or olive oil, as needed for sautéing

2 medallions North Australian (or other cold-water) lobster tail (8 to 10 ounces total)

3 cups wild mushrooms, chopped

8 cloves garlic

olive oil, as needed for roasting

1½ cups pearl onions and cipollini onions, peeled, sliced, and caramelized

1 bunch scallions, sliced

8 spears asparagus, grilled

LOBSTER SAUCE

2 tablespoons butter

2 tablespoons flour

olive oil, as needed

1 lobster shell, cut into large pieces

1 medium onion, chopped

1 fennel bulb, chopped

1 stalk celery, chopped

1 cup dry sherry

1 bay leaf

2 Roma tomatoes, pureed

8 cloves roasted garlic, reserved from filling

salt and pepper, to taste

CRUST

Cut butter into dry ingredients until texture resembles cornmeal. Add yogurt and water as needed, until crust comes together. Roll out dough and refrigerate until ready to use.

FILLING

Preheat oven to 400 degrees. Heat butter or oil in a large skillet over medium-high heat. Sauté lobster tail; remove from heat and chop into bite-size pieces. Spray or brush mushrooms and garlic with olive oil and roast in oven until mushrooms are soft. Reserve garlic. Place mushrooms, lobster meat, onions, scallions, and asparagus in a deep, ovenproof baking dish.

LOBSTER SAUCE

Prepare roux in a small saucepan by melting butter and whisking in flour. Cook until raw flour smell is gone; set aside. In a large pan sauté lobster shell, onion, fennel bulb, and celery in olive oil over medium heat until tender and nearly completely cooked. Deglaze pan with sherry. Add bay leaf, tomatoes, and reserved garlic, and reduce. Discard lobster shell and bay leaf. Add 2 tablespoons roux and season with salt and pepper.

Spoon enough sauce over meat and vegetables to cover. Top with a round of piecrust and press into rim of baking dish with fork. Cut two slashes in the top for steam vents and bake at 400 degrees until crust is nicely browned. Remove from oven and serve immediately.

Dijon- and Brown Sugar–Marinated Pork Tenderloin with Creamy Polenta and Andouille Sausage–Pear Compote

Tom Sheridan, LaSalle Grill (South Bend)

MARINATED PORK
½ cup soy sauce
¼ cup sherry vinegar
½ cup Dijon mustard
¼ cup brown sugar
1 branch fresh thyme
2 pork tenderloins (about 2 pounds total)

CREAMY POLENTA
2 cups whole milk
½ cup fine cornmeal
1 tablespoon butter
salt and pepper, to taste

COMPOTE
1 cup andouille sausage, chopped
½ onion, chopped
2 cups peeled, cored, and diced pear
1 cup chicken stock
1 branch thyme

MARINATED PORK

Combine first 5 ingredients in a large, zip-top plastic bag. Place pork loin in marinade, seal bag, and refrigerate for several hours.

CREAMY POLENTA

Bring milk to a boil and whisk in cornmeal. Lower heat and simmer gently until thick, about 30 minutes, stirring constantly. Whisk in butter and season with salt and pepper.

COMPOTE

Sauté sausage and onion in large pan over medium heat until sausage is no longer pink and onion is tender. Add pear and sauté. Deglaze pan with chicken stock. Add thyme and cook until pear begins to fall apart.

Grill pork to desired doneness on hot grill—160 degrees for medium, 180 degrees for well-done. Thinly slice into medallions.

Spoon ½ cup polenta onto each plate. Lay 4 to 5 slices pork loin in a half circle around the polenta, and top with compote.

Apple Fritters with Caramel Sauce

Lisa Sheridan, LaSalle Grill (South Bend)

CARAMEL SAUCE
2½ cups sugar
¼ teaspoon cream of tartar
½ cup water
2 cups heavy whipping cream

APPLE FRITTERS
1 egg
⅓ cup sugar
⅔ cup milk
2 tablespoons rum
1 tablespoon baking soda
1 teaspoon lemon zest
1 cup flour
4 apples, peeled and cored
oil, as needed for frying

ice cream

CARAMEL SAUCE

Combine first three ingredients in a medium saucepan and stir with fingers to incorporate fully. Place over medium-high heat and bring to a boil. Do not stir at this point, though you may swirl the pan every once in a while. Boil until the mixture is the color of dark caramel. Immediately add cream all at once. This will bubble profusely, so do it quickly and use caution. (Have a bowl of ice water nearby in case you are splashed with caramel sauce.) Lower heat to medium and whisk until all of sugar mixture is incorporated into caramel.

Remove from heat and set aside until ready to use. Caramel sauce can be refrigerated for up to 1 week. To reheat, place in a bain-marie (water bath) and slowly bring back to desired temperature.

APPLE FRITTERS

Mix together all ingredients except apples and set aside. Cut apples into ¼-inch slices. Dip slices in batter and fry in 375-degree oil in a deep fryer, heavy-bottomed pot, or deep skillet until golden on both sides. Serve with caramel sauce and ice cream.

Tad DeLay
Limestone Grille

LIMESTONE GRILLE
TAD DELAY, CHEF/OWNER
LINDA RIPPERGER, OWNER

2920 East Covenanter Drive
Bloomington, Indiana 47401

812-335-8110
www.limestonegrille.com

MENU

• Spicy Watermelon Salad

• Sweet Corn Pudding with Lobster

• Grilled Vegetables with Tamale
Pancakes and Pico de Gallo

• Fresh Blueberry and Lemon
Cream Tart

BEING THE CHEF-OWNER OF A fine-dining restaurant while keeping a second, more casual place running on the side is more than a full-time job by any estimate. When you ask Tad DeLay why he does it, he cracks a wry grin. "Because I'm nuts and I love it," he says. "I don't want to grow up and it keeps me young." He may be on to something—there is more than a touch of Peter Pan in DeLay. From the roguish light in his eye to the gleeful cackle of his laugh, he radiates youthful energy, good humor, and enjoyment in what he does.

Over the course of his twenty-eight years in the business, DeLay has honed a sure touch in the kitchen. He aims for a new American cuisine that is uncomplicated and that uses bold flavors to give common foods a new twist. His guiding

principle is to focus on quality ingredients and to keep the cooking simple. Dishes like salmon rubbed with fragrant ground chiles, grilled and served with a black bean and corn salsa, and grilled pork tenderloin with pear chutney and mashed potatoes are the delicious result.

As he creates a new dish, he is fascinated by the interplay of flavor and texture, with the ability of food to appeal to all the senses. He says, "People eat with their eyes first. If food looks good, they want to smell it. If it smells good, they want to taste it. If it tastes good, you've got them hooked."

DeLay came to cooking almost by accident, having studied biology and fine arts in college. Once he stumbled into restaurant work, however, he fell in love with what was happening in the kitchen, finding in food a new medium for his artistic talents.

His cooking experience has been gained at some venerable Indianapolis restaurants, working with Chef Edmond Goss at Meridian Hills Country Club, Don Caldwell at Adam's Rib in Zionsville, and Timothy Thomas at Thomas Caterers of Distinction. He was executive chef at Fletcher's American Grill and Café for four years.

Finally he and his wife, Linda Ripperger, decided that it was time to start working for themselves. Bloomington's diversity and small-town atmosphere captured their fancy, and in 1992 they bought Opie Taylor's, on Walnut Street. DeLay moved down to cook and run the place, and Ripperger kept her Indy job, doing the books on her weekend trips to Bloomington. In 1998 she quit and began planning the restaurant of their dreams—the Limestone Grille, which they finally opened a year later.

The finished product is a gorgeous sight to behold. Crisp white linens, green plants, and pale natural woods give the place a serene and elegant air. But capturing your eye from the moment you walk in is the masterpiece of the dining room, a wall-sized mosaic by artist Wendell Field made of 120 pieces of scrap Indiana limestone. It draws you across the room to run your hands over the stone, feeling the texture of rough against smooth. Field's work also appears on the patio where diners can eat outside in the warmer months.

Fortunately for diners, the artwork at the Limestone is not only on the walls. DeLay's food is as beautiful as it is delicious. These summer recipes are light and bright and breezy—perfect for a warm evening on the patio.

Spicy Watermelon Salad

Tad DeLay, Limestone Grille (Bloomington)

4 cups seedless watermelon balls or 1-inch cubes

4 scallions (green part only), sliced

2 cups peeled and diced jicama (this may also be scooped into balls with a melon baller)

1 cup fresh orange sections

1 jalapeño or other chile, seeded, deribbed, and diced very small

¼ cup champagne vinegar

¾ cup good-quality salad oil (e.g., Sterling)

salt and pepper, to taste

Bibb lettuce

Combine first 5 ingredients in medium mixing bowl and set aside. Put vinegar in small mixing bowl and slowly add oil, whisking continuously until emulsified. Season with salt and pepper. Drizzle vinaigrette on fruit mixture and toss until coated.

Line serving dishes with fresh Bibb lettuce cups. Place salad in center and serve.

Sweet Corn Pudding with Lobster

Tad DeLay, Limestone Grille (Bloomington)

2 to 3 ounces cooked lobster meat, picked clean of shell fragments and chopped

1 tablespoon butter, plus additional for greasing ramekins

4 ears in-season sweet corn, shucked

⅓ cup sugar

1 teaspoon salt

2 tablespoons all-purpose flour

2 large eggs, beaten

1 cup half and half

1 cup heavy whipping cream

salt and pepper, to taste

Preheat oven to 350 degrees. Lightly butter 4 6-ounce ramekins.

Stand ears of corn on end inside a shallow bowl and cut away kernels from cobs. Scrape cobs using back edge of knife to release sugar and cob milk. Add sugar, salt, and flour to corn and toss well.

In a bowl, mix eggs, half and half, and cream. Add to corn mixture. Season with salt and pepper.

Place 1 to 1½ tablespoons of lobster meat in the bottom of each ramekin and cover with corn mixture to three-fourths full. Place ramekins in a water bath reaching halfway up the ramekins and bake uncovered for 40 minutes, or until custard is just set.

Grilled Vegetables with Tamale Pancakes and Pico de Gallo

Tad DeLay, Limestone Grille (Bloomington)

GRILLED VEGETABLES

2 large zucchini, washed and sliced lengthwise to ¼-inch thickness

2 large yellow squash, washed and sliced lengthwise to ¼-inch thickness

1 large Vidalia onion, peeled and sliced to ¼-inch thickness

1 pound fresh asparagus, washed and trimmed 3 inches up from stem end

2 large portobello mushroom caps, brushed clean

1 cup extra-virgin olive oil

salt and pepper, to taste

PICO DE GALLO

4 ripe tomatoes, seeded and diced small

1 medium red onion, peeled and diced small

2 chile peppers, seeded, deribbed and diced small

juice of 4 limes

4 tablespoons chopped fresh cilantro

salt and pepper, to taste

TAMALE PANCAKES

4½ cups diced tomatillos

1½ cups whole milk

1 cup masa harina (fine cornmeal for making tortillas)

1 cup diced red bell pepper

¾ cup sliced green onion

¼ cup chopped fresh cilantro

¼ teaspoon baking soda

1½ tablespoons butter

butter or oil, as needed for cooking pancakes

GRILLED VEGETABLES

Lay vegetable slices flat on sheet pans. Brush generously with olive oil and season with salt and pepper. Set aside.

PICO DE GALLO

Combine first 5 ingredients in a medium mixing bowl and toss to coat. Season with salt and pepper. Set aside in refrigerator.

TAMALE PANCAKES

Place tomatillos, milk, and masa harina in a medium, thick-bottomed sauce pan. Place pan over medium-high heat, stirring frequently until mixture has thickened. Remove mixture from stove and add red bell pepper, green onions, cilantro, baking soda, and butter. Stir until combined. Let cool completely. (This batter can be made up to 8 hours in advance.)

Light grill and bring to medium-high heat. While grill is heating, prepare tamale pancakes on stovetop. Make pancakes about 4 inches in diameter and ¾ inch thick. Fry in butter or oil in large cast iron or aluminum skillet over medium heat until golden brown on both sides and done in the center. Keep prepared pancakes warm in 200-degree oven until vegetables are grilled.

Grill vegetables until almost cooked through on both sides.

Arrange vegetables on each plate. Place pancake at bottom of each plate, partially overlapping vegetables. Top with pico de gallo.

Fresh Blueberry and Lemon Cream Tart

Serves 12

Tad DeLay, Limestone Grille (Bloomington)

PASTRY
2 cups all-purpose flour

¼ cup extra-fine sugar

½ teaspoon baking powder

¼ teaspoon salt

1 stick butter, cubed and cold

2 large eggs, lightly beaten

FILLING
1½ pints fresh blueberries

3 tablespoons extra-fine sugar

¼ cup crème de cassis

¾ cup heavy whipping cream

1½ jars lemon curd

PASTRY
Combine dry ingredients in a medium mixing bowl. Cut in butter until it resembles coarse grain. Add eggs and work them in with your hands until pastry starts to form a ball. Turn out pastry onto floured work area and knead four times only. Form into disk, wrap, and refrigerate for 2 hours.

FILLING
Preheat oven to 350 degrees. Rinse blueberries and place in a medium mixing bowl with sugar and crème de cassis; toss and set aside. Whip cream by hand or with electric mixer until stiff peaks form. Put lemon curd in a small bowl and whip to loosen it. Mix cream into lemon curd. Set aside and refrigerate.

To finish tart, roll pastry into a 16-inch diameter circle. Roll it onto rolling pin and drape over an 11-inch fluted tart pan with removable bottom. Settle pastry into pan with fingers. Gently roll rolling pin across the top of the pan, cutting pastry. (Freeze extra pastry for future use.) Prick pastry with fork.

Place in oven and bake until golden brown, about 10 to 15 minutes. Remove and cool to room temperature.

Spread lemon cream evenly across bottom of tart pan to about halfway up sides of pastry. Drain berries, arrange evenly on top of cream, and serve.

Brannon Soileau

Maize,
An American Grill

MAIZE, AN AMERICAN GRILL
Brannon and Christie Soileau,
Proprietors
Brannon Soileau, Chef

112 North 3rd Street
Lafayette, Indiana 47901

765-429-6125
www.maizeinc.com

MENU

• **Indiana Corn and Potato Chowder**

• **Buffalo Rock Shrimp Salad with Roasted Indiana Corn Relish and Maytag Blue-Cheese Dressing**

• **Skewered Salmon on Indiana Corn Cake with Shagbark Hickory Glaze**

• **Blackened Ribeye on a Double-Stuffed Potato with Grilled Vegetables**

BRANNON SOILEAU FIZZES AND POPS when he talks about food and cooking and his Lafayette restaurant, Maize, An American Grill. His compact body can barely contain his enthusiasm, and his snappy, picturesque language paints a colorful, wrenchingly honest self portrait. For all his energy, though, he is a man who seems supremely comfortable with his life—both where he has been and where he is headed.

Soileau got turned onto the exciting possibilities of food by his mom. She was a good Southern cook,

and—his football coach dad often away from home through much of his childhood—Brannon spent long hours in her southern Louisiana kitchen watching her turn out gumbos, pot roasts, and great fried chicken.

His fascination with food helped rescue him when, as a young man, he was unable to settle on a college major or a career path. During those "lost years" he was "always cooking, all the time," thriving on the camaraderie, the ever-changing action, the heat, and the stress of high-powered kitchen work. An older friend who knew about his fondness for cooking took him under his wing, mentoring him and urging him to take it to a new level by enrolling in the Culinary Institute of America in upstate New York.

Soileau knew it was time for him to get serious, and he gave it everything he had, making the Dean's List for the first time in his life, determined to succeed. "I rocked," he says of his years at the CIA, and he came away with new energy, creative focus, and a wife—pastry chef Christie. An externship in the Cayman Islands with Chef Erhard Tell was followed by stints in the restaurants of the Four Seasons hotel chain in Chicago, Austin, San Francisco, and Dallas, working on the line and as sous chef.

All the hard work and travel paid off and he was offered the executive chef position at the 480-seat Pump Room in Chicago, where he worked "like a damn dog" for two years. But by then Christie had had a baby and Brannon was working furiously all the time. Eventually they knew it was time to stop working for other people and to make a move. They settled on downtown Lafayette, where they were drawn to the diversity of the town and the beauty of the courthouse square.

Their restaurant, Maize, truly is an American grill. Soileau's goal is for Midwesterners to enter his restaurant, named for that all-American grain, and find the foods they grew up with, but with a twist. Stalwarts on the menu include the popular pecan-crusted catfish with chile-lime sauce, massive grilled steaks and slow roasted pork loin with Jack Daniel's jalapeño honey sauce and sweet potato hash browns.

Does he ever tempt patrons with Cajun cooking? "I give them my blood and they love it," he says, "but I do it as specials." Specials give him the chance to have fun with the menu and try out new ideas, to put to good use the fact that he is thinking about food all the time, trying to put fresh, seasonal Indiana ingredients onto the plate in a way that will excite all the senses, and send his customers home comfortable and happy.

His late-fall menu showcases the Maize approach to food—solid Midwestern ingredients (huge steaks, lots of corn!), but with an innovative and contemporary twist.

Indiana Corn and Potato Chowder

Brannon Soileau, Maize, An American Grill (Lafayette)

½ cup all-purpose flour

8 tablespoons (1 stick) butter, melted

1½ pounds applewood-smoked bacon

3 tablespoons corn oil

3 cups chopped Spanish onions

½ cup chopped celery

2 cups chopped bell peppers (a mix of red, green, and yellow)

¼ cup minced garlic

3 cups corn, sliced off cob, cobs reserved

6 cups chicken or vegetable stock

3 cups heavy cream

1 teaspoon chopped fresh thyme

2 bay leaves

2 cups chopped Yukon Gold potatoes

salt and pepper, to taste

sugar, to taste, as needed

roasted red peppers, pureed, as garnish (optional)

Make roux by mixing flour and butter together in a medium saucepan until it resembles sand. Over medium heat cook and stir for about 5 minutes. Do not let roux develop any color. Set aside to cool.

In large pot, cook bacon in corn oil until fairly crispy and fat is rendered. Add onion, celery, peppers, garlic, and corn and sauté until onions are translucent. Do not let vegetables brown. Add stock, cream, thyme, bay leaves, and reserved corncobs. Simmer 20 minutes.

Add potatoes and cook until tender. Add roux little by little, until soup thickens just enough to coat the back of the spoon. Remove cobs and bay leaves. Once thickened, simmer 10 minutes. Season with salt and pepper. Add sugar if corn is not sweet enough. Drizzle with red pepper puree, if desired. Serve.

Buffalo Rock Shrimp Salad with Roasted Indiana Corn Relish and Maytag Blue-Cheese Dressing

Serves 4 to 6

Brannon Soileau, Maize, An American Grill (Lafayette)

CORN RELISH

4 ears Indiana sweet corn, roasted in husks on medium-hot to hot grill or in 400-degree oven until tender

1 red bell pepper, diced

1 green bell pepper, diced

¼ cup corn oil

¼ cup lime juice

3 tablespoons chopped cilantro

¼ cup minced red onion

3 tablespoons minced garlic

ground cumin, to taste

salt and pepper, to taste

sugar, to taste, as needed

MAYTAG BLUE-CHEESE DRESSING

1 pound Maytag blue cheese, crumbled

1 cup hot water

2 cups mayonnaise

¼ cup lemon juice

¼ cup heavy cream

¼ cup chopped chives

salt and cracked black pepper, to taste

BUFFALO SAUCE

16 tablespoons (2 sticks) butter

2 cups barbecue sauce

1 cup sambal oelek chili sauce (available in Asian markets)

salt and pepper, to taste

ROCK SHRIMP

5 cups corn oil

4 cups all-purpose flour

salt and pepper, to taste

3 eggs

2½ cups buttermilk

1 pound rock shrimp

3 romaine hearts, chopped

½ pound field greens

4 Roma tomatoes, cleaned and quartered

CORN RELISH

Carefully peel back corn husks; remove silk and close husks. Roast on medium-hot to hot grill, turning frequently, until corn is tender and first layer of husk is charred. (Alternately, roast in a 400-degree oven until corn is tender.) Remove and let cool. Cut kernels from cob. Combine corn with other ingredients and set aside. (Relish is best made a day ahead or early in the morning so that flavors can marry.)

MAYTAG BLUE-CHEESE DRESSING

Stir together all ingredients and set aside.

BUFFALO SAUCE

Melt butter in a medium saucepan over medium heat. Add remaining ingredients, heat, and set aside, keeping sauce warm.

ROCK SHRIMP

Heat oil to 350 degrees. Combine flour, salt, and pepper. Whisk together eggs and buttermilk. Roll shrimp in seasoned flour, dip in buttermilk mixture, and then roll in seasoned flour again. Fry until golden brown. Drain on paper towel. Toss shrimp in buffalo sauce.

To serve, toss greens in blue-cheese dressing to taste. (Reserve excess dressing in refrigerator for future use.) Top with corn relish and buffalo shrimp. Garnish with tomatoes.

Skewered Salmon on Indiana Corn Cake
with Shagbark Hickory Glaze

Serves 6

Brannon Soileau, Maize, An American Grill (Lafayette)

SHAGBARK HICKORY GLAZE

oil, as needed

1 tablespoon chopped garlic

1 tablespoon crushed red pepper flakes

1 tablespoon chopped fresh thyme

2 cups shagbark hickory syrup (see Sources)

INDIANA CORN CAKE

2 teaspoons yeast

1¼ cup milk, warm

1 ear Indiana sweet corn, roasted in husks over medium-hot to hot grill or in 400-degree oven until tender

1 cup cornmeal

1 cup all-purpose flour

1 teaspoon salt, plus additional to taste

2 tablespoons (¼ stick) butter, melted

2 eggs

white pepper, to taste

oil, as needed

VEGETABLES

1 pound French green beans

1 cup corn relish (see recipe for Buffalo Rock Shrimp Salad on p. 66)

1 pound fresh spinach

butter or oil, as needed

salt and pepper, to taste

SKEWERED SALMON

6 8-ounce salmon fillets, each cut into 4 strips

reserved shagbark hickory glaze

SHAGBARK HICKORY GLAZE

Heat small amount of oil in a small saucepan over medium heat. Briefly sauté garlic, red pepper, and thyme. Add syrup and bring to hard simmer for a few minutes, until mixture coats the back of the spoon. Set aside for glazing salmon during grilling; reserve small portion for finishing plates before serving.

INDIANA CORN CAKE

Bloom yeast in milk until soft. Cut corn kernels from cob and combine with cornmeal, flour, salt, butter, and eggs. Stir in yeast mixture; consistency should resemble that of pancake batter. Season well with additional salt and white pepper. Let batter rest for 30 minutes. Cook six large corn cakes in small amount of oil in a large pan over medium heat until both sides are golden brown.

VEGETABLES

Cook beans in boiling salted water until tender but still crunchy. In a large pan over medium heat, sauté corn relish, spinach, and beans in small amount of butter or oil until vegetables are warmed and spinach is wilted. Season with salt and pepper.

SKEWERED SALMON

Light grill and bring to medium-high heat. Thread salmon strips lengthwise on metal skewers or on bamboo skewers that have been soaked in water. Grill salmon, brushing often with shagbark hickory glaze and turning frequently. Salmon is done when it is opaque and firm but not dry.

Serve with corn cake in center of plate, topped with vegetables. Lean 4 skewers on vegetables. Drizzle reserved glaze on top of salmon and around plate.

Blackened Ribeye on a Double-Stuffed Potato with Grilled Vegetables

Serves 4

Brannon Soileau, Maize, An American Grill (Lafayette)

BLACK PEPPER–HORSERADISH CREAM

1½ cups sour cream

1½ tablespoons fresh cracked black pepper

2½ tablespoons prepared horseradish

¼ cup heavy whipping cream

2 tablespoons lemon juice

GRILLED VEGETABLES

1 zucchini, top and bottom cut off, sliced lengthwise down center

1 squash, top and bottom cut off, sliced lengthwise down center

1 red bell pepper, seeded and halved

1 small red onion, sliced ½-inch thick

2 carrots, peeled and cut lengthwise into thirds

¼ cup olive oil

salt and pepper, to taste

DOUBLE-STUFFED POTATO

2 Idaho baking potatoes, baked in 450-degree oven until tender

2 Idaho baking potatoes, peeled, quartered, boiled until tender, and drained

8 tablespoons (1 stick) butter, at room temperature

1 cup heavy whipping cream, hot

½ cup sour cream

2 cups shredded Vermont white cheddar cheese

¼ cup chopped chives

salt and pepper, to taste

BLACKENED RIBEYE

4 26-ounce bone-in ribeye steaks

salt and pepper, to taste

1½ cups Cajun blackening seasoning

¼ cup corn oil

butter or oil, as needed

2 cups fresh spinach

salt and pepper, to taste

BLACK PEPPER–HORSERADISH CREAM

Stir together all ingredients and refrigerate until ready to use.

GRILLED VEGETABLES

Brush or toss vegetables with olive oil and season with salt and pepper. Grill over medium to high heat or broil in oven. Cook until vegetables reach light color; bake carrot and red onion further in a 375-degree oven, as needed, until tender. Let vegetables cool immediately; do not stack. Once cool, cut in large chunks and set aside.

DOUBLE-STUFFED POTATO

Halve baked potatoes lengthwise and scoop out pulp, reserving potato shells. Place potato pulp and boiled potatoes in a large bowl and follow your favorite procedure for mashing potatoes, adding butter, cream, sour cream, cheese, and chives until potatoes have a smooth,

creamy texture. (More or less of these ingredients may be necessary depending on the moisture content of the potatoes.) Season with salt and pepper. Pipe or spoon warm potato mixture into baked potato shells and refrigerate until set. When ready to serve, heat in 375-degree oven for 15 to 20 minutes or until brown on top and warm through center.

Blackened Ribeye

Pat steaks dry with paper towel. Season with salt and pepper. Place seasoning on plate and press both sides of each steak into seasoning. Liberally coat both sides of steaks with oil. Heat a cast iron or heavy-bottomed, oven-safe pan over very high heat. Place steaks in pan and sear 3 to 4 minutes per side. Seasoning will turn black, but do not let it scorch or burn. (There will be a strong smell so activate exhaust fan or open windows.) Finish in 375-degree oven until desired temperature is reached.

As steaks are finishing, warm mixed cut vegetables in a small amount of butter or oil with spinach in a large pan over medium heat until spinach is wilted. Season with salt and pepper.

Serve steak over double-stuffed potato with grilled vegetables and black pepper–horseradish cream to the side.

(Tip: Timing is everything with this dish. Put double-stuffed potatoes in oven just before starting steaks. As the steaks are finishing in the oven, sauté grilled vegetables.)

Gary Sanders
Miller Bakery Café

MILLER BAKERY CAFÉ

GARY SANDERS, CHEF AND
PROPRIETOR

555 Lake Street
Gary, Indiana 46403

219-938-2229

MENU

• **Petite Lobster "BLT"**

• **Olive Oil–Poached Salmon and
Heirloom Tomatoes**

• **Australian Rack of Lamb with
Black Truffle Potatoes**

• **Bittersweet Chocolate Marquise
with Chambord Raspberries**

FOR GARY SANDERS COOKING IS ALL
about eating. When he talks about food, he talks
about what he likes to eat, great meals he has
had, exotic places he travels to eat. He is, he says,
"addicted to food,"—part of the high-energy
intensity of this self-admitted workaholic.

Sanders got interested in food as a kid, when
he took a cooking class in high school, thinking it
would be a blow-off class that wouldn't tax him
too much. He surprised himself by liking it, and
did well enough to get the attention of the teacher,
who suggested he go to culinary school.

He flirted with the idea of following his dad into the asbestos-removal business, but a brief trial convinced him that "that toxic lifestyle" was not for him. Meanwhile, he had been working as a busboy in a country club, and always "poking his nose" into the kitchen to see what the chefs were doing. The food and the creative energy there fascinated him, and he found the adrenalin of the kitchen culture addictive even as a busboy.

He headed to culinary school, and eventually applied for a job at The Cottage, an acclaimed restaurant in Calumet City, Illinois, just so he could meet his idol, Chef Carolyn Buster. To his surprise, he got the job, and moved up the ladder quickly to become the sous chef, learning many facets of the restaurant business—from how to work with new ingredients like porcini mushrooms to ordering high-quality food. The two-and-a-half years he spent in Buster's kitchen taught him a lot, but still he was scarcely prepared for his next venture.

When he was twenty-two, he took on the job of head chef at the newly-opened Miller Bakery Café and found himself out of his depth almost immediately. He struggled to create a menu that had no connection with The Cottage and found it took several years before he developed his own cooking style.

When that style developed, it was as eclectic as the restaurant's mix-and-match china, incorporating Italian/Mediterranean foods and ingredients with a Midwestern sensibility. What he had learned from Buster was not to push people outside of their food comfort zone before they were ready. He tries hard to earn his customers' respect, knowing that once they trust him to cook delicious food, they will try new things more readily.

Eventually he ended up buying the restaurant, and seems to have found restaurant ownership as addictive as food and kitchen work, since he's been adding new places to his list ever since. He calls himself a project fanatic who gets bored easily, but despite his growing empire, the Miller Bakery Café is his baby, and he puts time in there every day.

Today his food is innovative without being too tricked out. He says he is not interested in seeing how far you can take a duck breast from being a duck breast, or how weird you can get with fusion. Instead the flavors in his cooking are complex and layered without getting cluttered, as he demonstrates in this gorgeous summer menu.

Petite Lobster "BLT"

Serves 6

Gary Sanders, Miller Bakery Café (Gary)

Saffron-Tarragon Aïoli

¼ cup white wine

1 teaspoon fresh tarragon, chopped

pinch saffron threads

2 teaspoons chopped shallots

1 teaspoon lemon zest

juice of ½ lemon

1 teaspoon chopped or pressed garlic

½ cup prepared mayonnaise

salt and white pepper, to taste

Sandwich

12 slices brioche

3 tablespoons unsalted butter, softened

6 slices applewood-smoked bacon, cooked
   until slightly crisp

2 vine-ripened Roma tomatoes, sliced

1 cup fresh arugula, washed and stemmed

1 cup cooked lobster meat, picked clean
   of shell fragments

12 herb sprigs

lemon zest, optional, for garnish

arugula leaves, optional, for garnish

Saffron-Tarragon Aïoli

In a medium, non-reactive saucepan, cook first 7 ingredients (wine through garlic) over medium heat until liquid is reduced to 1 tablespoon. Remove from heat and cool slightly. Place mayonnaise in food processor and add tarragon mixture. Process until smooth and strain through fine sieve. Chill until ready to use. (This may be prepared one day ahead.)

Sandwich

Using a 3-inch round food mold or biscuit cutter, cut 2 circles out of each slice of brioche, or cut into 3-inch squares; discard crusts. Spread each side with a small amount of butter. In a large non-stick skillet over medium heat, toast brioche on both sides and remove from pan.

Preheat oven to 325 degrees. Lay half of the toasted brioche circles on a clean surface. On each piece of brioche, place ⅓ slice bacon, 1 slice tomato, and a few leaves of arugula. Place a portion of lobster on top and press down slightly. Drizzle small amount of aïoli and top each circle with remaining piece of brioche. Skewer each sandwich with herb sprig to hold together.

Place sandwiches on a sheet tray and heat slightly in oven for 3 to 4 minutes. Remove from tray and place on serving platter. Garnish with lemon zest or additional arugula leaves.

Olive Oil–Poached Salmon and Heirloom Tomatoes

Gary Sanders, Miller Bakery Café (Gary)

PINOT NOIR VINAIGRETTE

4 ounces pinot noir

2 ounces extra virgin olive oil

2 ounces grapeseed oil

2 tablespoons light brown sugar

¼ teaspoon ground star anise

1 medium shallot, finely chopped

1 clove garlic, finely chopped or pressed

pinch fleur de sel (sea salt)

freshly cracked black pepper, to taste

SALMON AND TOMATOES

12 small to medium assorted ripened heirloom tomatoes

6 to 8 4-ounce salmon fillets, skin and pin bones removed

2 cups extra-virgin olive oil, or more as needed

sprigs of fresh thyme, to taste

2 cloves garlic, sliced

ARUGULA SALAD

1 pound fresh arugula, washed and stemmed

1 small red onion, peeled, slivered, and marinated in small amount of pinot noir vinaigrette (above) for 1 hour

freshly cracked black pepper, for garnish

thyme sprigs, for garnish

PINOT NOIR VINAIGRETTE

Place all ingredients in blender and blend 1 minute. Strain through fine sieve and refrigerate 1 to 2 hours. (This can be made 1 to 2 days ahead of time.)

SALMON AND TOMATOES

Cut tops off tomatoes and discard. Place tomatoes and salmon fillets in a shallow-sided saucepan. Add olive oil to cover, then add thyme and garlic. Heat oil to 225 to 250 degrees and cover pan. Poach salmon and tomatoes in oil 20 to 25 minutes, based on thickness of salmon. Salmon is done when firm to the touch; be careful not to overcook.

Remove saucepan from heat and allow fillets and tomatoes to cool slightly in poaching oil. Carefully remove tomatoes from oil and set on cutting board. Remove any remaining skin and slice in half. Remove and discard any seeds. Keep tomatoes warm by placing back in poaching oil.

ARUGULA SALAD

Remove red onion from vinaigrette. Toss arugula in half of remaining vinaigrette. Create a nest of greens in center of each plate. Carefully remove salmon fillets from oil and place atop arugula. Divide poached tomatoes, placing equal amounts around each salad. Drizzle a small amount of remaining vinaigrette around each salad. Place marinated red onions atop salmon fillets and garnish with pepper and thyme sprigs. Serve immediately.

Australian Rack of Lamb with Black Truffle Potatoes

Serves 6 to 8

Gary Sanders, Miller Bakery Café (Gary)

ROSEMARY-INFUSED LAMB SAUCE

olive oil, as needed

2 teaspoons minced garlic

2 teaspoons minced shallot

2 teaspoons finely chopped fresh rosemary sprigs (or 1 teaspoon dried)

cracked black pepper, to taste

4 cups red wine (zinfandel, cabernet, or other full-bodied red wine)

4 cups seasoned lamb stock (or substitute veal stock)

4 tablespoons tomato puree or 2 tablespoons tomato paste

1 tablespoon white truffle oil

AUSTRALIAN RACK OF LAMB

4 8-bone racks of Australian lamb (or substitute New Zealand lamb), French-boned (shin bones left in and cleaned by scraping away from loin with sharp knife)

¼ cup olive oil

2 tablespoons finely chopped garlic

2 tablespoons finely chopped fresh rosemary

¼ cup red wine

coarse salt and freshly cracked black pepper, to taste

BLACK TRUFFLE POTATOES

10 large Yukon Gold potatoes, peeled and quartered

4 tablespoons extra-virgin olive oil

2 tablespoons unsalted butter

1 teaspoon black truffle peelings, finely chopped (or substitute 2 tablespoons truffle butter for unsalted butter and truffle peelings)

¼ cup heavy whipping cream

1 teaspoon white truffle-infused oil

fleur de sel (sea salt) and freshly cracked black pepper, to taste

rosemary sprig, for garnish

fleur de sel (sea salt), for garnish

freshly cracked black pepper, for garnish

julienne-cut vegetables, lightly stir-fried, for garnish

Rosemary-Infused Lamb Sauce

In a large, nonreactive saucepan over medium heat, heat olive oil, garlic, shallots, rosemary, and pepper. Add wine and reduce by half, about 12 minutes. Add stock and tomato product. Reduce by half and adjust seasonings. Whisk in truffle oil and keep warm. (This may be made 1 to 2 days ahead of time and slowly reheated before serving.)

Australian Rack of Lamb

Trim excess fat from lamb and score remaining fat to aid rendering. Cut each rack in half, being careful to cut through joints. In large bowl, whisk together remaining ingredients. Lay each portion of lamb flat in non-reactive container. Pour marinade over lamb. Cover and refrigerate for 4 to 6 hours or overnight.

Black Truffle Potatoes

Place potatoes in a medium saucepan, cover with water, and bring to boil. Continue cooking potatoes until tender, 15 to 18 minutes. In small saucepan, heat olive oil, butter, truffle peelings, and cream. Follow your favorite procedure for mashing potatoes, adding olive oil mixture in small amounts until incorporated. When potatoes are smooth, finish with truffle oil, salt, and pepper.

Prepare lamb directly over medium-hot grill or roast in 400-degree oven in a roasting pan. Cook lamb until desired temperature is reached, turning occasionally and being careful not to burn the bones. Remove lamb from grill or oven and let rest for 10 to 12 minutes.

To serve, place a dollop of potatoes in the center of each plate. Slice lamb rack into individual chops and lay atop potatoes. Ladle generous amount of sauce around lamb. Garnish with rosemary sprig, stir-fried vegetables, sprinkle of salt, and touch of pepper.

Bittersweet Chocolate Marquise with Chambord Raspberries

Serves 6 to 8

Gary Sanders, Miller Bakery Café (Gary)

CHOCOLATE MARQUISE

21 tablespoons (2⅝ sticks) unsalted butter, divided

12 ounces imported bittersweet chocolate, chopped

7 egg whites

CHAMBORD RASPBERRIES

½ pint fresh raspberries

3 tablespoons sugar

2 ounces Chambord (black raspberry liqueur)

FRANGELICO CRÈME ANGLAISE

6 egg yolks

1 cup sugar

2 cups heavy whipping cream

2 cups whole milk

1 tablespoon vanilla extract

2 tablespoons cornstarch, dissolved in 2 tablespoons milk

2 ounces Frangelico (hazelnut liqueur)

fresh mint, for garnish

CHOCOLATE MARQUISE

Spread a medium loaf pan or similar container with 1 tablespoon softened butter. Carefully line pan with plastic wrap, overlapping sides 3 or 4 inches all around. This will help when removing marquise from pan. Set aside.

In a double boiler, melt remaining butter and chocolate together until smooth. Remove from heat and set aside. In clean stainless steel bowl, whip egg whites until stiff peaks form. Slowly fold whites into chocolate mixture until completely incorporated. Pour mixture into prepared pan and cover with plastic wrap. Refrigerate 3 to 4 hours or until completely firm. (This may be prepared ahead of time and refrigerated for 2 days or frozen for several weeks.)

CHAMBORD RASPBERRIES

Carefully pick through raspberries, discarding any with spots or mold. Set aside. In a medium, nonreactive mixing bowl, whisk together sugar and Chambord until smooth. Carefully fold in raspberries. Cover and refrigerate for 1 to 2 hours before serving.

FRANGELICO CRÈME ANGLAISE

Whisk together egg yolks and sugar in medium bowl. Set aside. In medium, heavy-bottomed saucepan, bring cream, milk, and vanilla to boil. Pour small amount into egg mixture to temper and whisk quickly, being careful not to cook eggs. Pour egg mixture into cream mixture and return to stovetop. Cook until thickened (do not boil). Whisk in dissolved cornstarch and reheat. If mixture is too thin, add additional cornstarch. If mixture is too thick, add small amount of milk. Remove from heat and strain through fine sieve. Place in ice water bath to chill quickly. When cooled, stir in Frangelico. Refrigerate until ready to serve.

To serve, remove marquise from pan by running the bottom of the pan under hot water for a few seconds, being careful not to melt chocolate. Remove top layer of plastic wrap and place pan upside down on a flat surface. Firmly grip overlapped plastic wrap and lift pan; marquise should slide out. Remove remaining plastic and smooth out marquise with a knife or spatula dipped in hot water.

Transfer to serving dish or slice and divide among plates. Pour Frangelico crème anglaise around marquise and spoon raspberries over the top. Garnish with fresh mint and serve.

Steven Oakley
Oakleys Bistro

OAKLEYS BISTRO
Steven Oakley,
Chef-Proprietor

1464 West 86th Street
Indianapolis, Indiana 46260

317-824-1231
www.oakleysbistro.com

MENU

- Lobster and Duck

- Shrimp Corndogs

- Salmon with Prosciutto Crust and Plum-Cilantro Relish

- Char-Grilled Quail with Figs and Balsamic-Honey Glaze

TRYING TO ARRANGE AN INTERVIEW with a chef after he's been written up in *Bon Appétit* is a challenge. In the days following the magazine's publication, Oakleys Bistro was packed, cranking up the pressure and causing Chef Steve Oakley to say somewhat plaintively that while he enjoys the attention, "We just want to serve good food and good wine and have fun."

Despite the national reputation, that's what he manages to do. Serving good food is

in Oakley's blood—his grandparents had a store and deli when he was young. He cooked with his mom and grandmother through high school, and watched plenty of Graham Kerr and Julia Child on TV. Although he was heavily into sports as a kid, he knew that wasn't going to be his life's work, and when it was time to think about a career, cooking looked good.

When he was sixteen he went to work at The Cottage, a four-star restaurant in Calumet City, Illinois, where he was so thrilled to learn classical French cooking from Chef Carolyn Buster that he was willing to work for free. After four years there he enrolled at the Culinary Institute of America, followed by a stint at the Scottsdale Princess, in Arizona, and then a year at Charlie Trotter's in Chicago.

Trotter's was a valuable experience for the twenty-year-old chef; it taught him that he wasn't interested in composing a meal consisting of separate little bites, but wanted to focus instead on planning the whole meal. He worked at Chicago's Printer's Row under Chef Michael Foley, before landing in Indianapolis—first at Benvenuti for a year, and then for a longer stretch at Something Different that ended with him taking over as chef.

After years of working in other people's kitchens, Oakley felt that it was time to create one of his own. Two years in the planning, Oakleys Bistro gives him the chance to craft the dining experience he believes people in Indianapolis should be able to have—great quality food and wine you don't have to pay through the nose for. Every detail of the experience is carefully planned, down to the black shirts of the busboys, the blue shirts of the servers, the pewter water pitchers, and the landscaping outside the front door that gives the illusion of garden dining in the midst of an upscale strip mall.

As he talks about his restaurant, Oakley's cool light eyes are intense. This is a project he has a fierce commitment to. He wants to create a restaurant that draws people for more than just one reason, hence patrons come for lunch, dinner, carry-out, cooking classes, the chef-of-the-day experiences, wine dinners, or just a drink at the bar.

But, truthfully, mostly they come for the food. Oakley's style has evolved through the years, to be simpler—more local, more seasonal, but more whimsical and fun as well. Shrimp corndogs, for instance, are a classy take on an old carnival favorite; "lobster and duck" is a terse, abbreviated name for a rich dish that is complex and layered in flavor. Oakley focuses on technique and proper cooking methods, getting back to basics in a simple but elegant way by providing a different gloss on comfort classics, like duck pot pie, buttermilk-fried quail, or meatloaf with a barbeque glaze. The menu he provides here is just what he aims for—fresh and delicious food prepared in a playful and innovative way.

Lobster and Duck

Steven Oakley, Oakleys Bistro (Indianapolis)

CRÊPES

4 tablespoons (½ stick) butter

½ cup flour

2 eggs

½ cup milk

pinch of salt

pinch of pepper

6 ounces lobster tail meat

6 ounces duck confit (duck meat cooked and preserved in its rendered fat; or substitute roasted, pulled duck meat)

cucumber, diced, for garnish

tomato concassée (peeled, seeded, and diced tomatoes), for garnish

micro greens, for garnish

cracked mustard seeds, for garnish

truffle oil, for garnish

shellfish oil, optional, for garnish

CRÊPES

Melt butter. Place remaining ingredients in blender with butter and puree until smooth. Heat 10-inch nonstick sauté pan over medium heat until warm. Add 1 ounce batter, swirling pan to cover evenly, and cook until dry. Repeat with remaining batter, and set aside.

In a shallow skillet, heat enough water or other poaching liquid just to cover lobster tail. When liquid reaches gentle simmer, add lobster tail and poach until medium-rare; flesh should change color and be firm but not rubbery. Remove from heat and slice as desired.

Fill crêpes with confit and plate with lobster tail. Garnish with cucumber, tomato concassée, micro greens, and cracked mustard seeds. Drizzle with oils. Warm in oven on cedar board and serve.

Shrimp Corndogs

Steven Oakley, Oakleys Bistro (Indianapolis)

Bistro Honey Mustard
1 cup honey
2 tablespoons Dijon mustard

Cornmeal Batter
1 cup plus 2 tablespoons cornmeal
2 cups all-purpose flour
¼ cup sugar
1 tablespoon baking powder
2 cups milk
1 egg yolk
1 egg
1 cup fresh corn, chopped

10 to 15 large shrimp, peeled, deveined, and tails removed

oil, as needed for deep-frying
wooden skewers

Bistro Honey Mustard
Combine honey and mustard and reserve.

Cornmeal Batter
Combine all ingredients in a large bowl. As batter sits, cornmeal will swell; add additional milk as needed to thin batter.

Skewer 1 shrimp, dip into batter, and fry in 340-degree oil until golden brown. Repeat with remaining shrimp. Serve with honey mustard.

Salmon with Prosciutto Crust and Plum-Cilantro Relish

Serves 4

Steven Oakley, Oakleys Bistro (Indianapolis)

PLUM-CILANTRO RELISH
3 cups sliced plums
2 shallots, minced
1 stalk celery, chopped
1 tablespoon chopped cilantro
1 tablespoon olive oil
lime juice, to taste

4 thin slices prosciutto
2 bunches baby spinach, washed
4 6-ounce center-cut salmon fillets
salt and pepper, to taste
olive oil, as needed

cracked mustard seeds, for garnish

PLUM-CILANTRO RELISH
Combine all 6 ingredients and reserve.

Preheat oven to 350 degrees. Bake prosciutto on parchment paper 8 to 10 minutes, or until crispy. Dry on paper towel and reserve.

Quickly sauté spinach in one teaspoon of olive oil until just wilted. Season with salt and pepper.

Heat oil in a large skillet over medium-high heat. Season salmon with salt and pepper and sear to desired temperature.

Serve salmon with spinach and topped with crispy prosciutto, plum-cilantro relish, and cracked mustard seeds.

Char-Grilled Quail with Figs and Balsamic-Honey Glaze

Steven Oakley, Oakleys Bistro (Indianapolis)

BALSAMIC HONEY GLAZE

2 tablespoons balsamic vinegar

3 to 4 tablespoons honey

1 jalapeño pepper, seeded and diced

4 leaves basil, thinly sliced

1 tablespoon finely minced chives

SALAD

1 tablespoon butter

1 tablespoon olive oil

1 leek (white part only), julienned

1 carrot, julienned

1 cup julienned fennel bulb

¼ cup julienne-cut radishes

4 semi-boneless quail

salt and pepper, to taste

4 to 6 fresh figs, for garnish

micro greens, for garnish

BALSAMIC-HONEY GLAZE

Reduce balsamic vinegar to syrup over low heat. Add remaining ingredients and reserve.

SALAD

Place butter and olive oil in a large skillet over medium heat. When butter has melted, sauté leek, carrot, radishes, and fennel bulb until tender.

Light grill and bring to high heat. French-bone quail (i.e., leave in, but trim, wing and thigh bones) and season with salt and pepper. Grill skin side down until well browned, 6 to 7 minutes. Turn and cook quail until juices run clear when thigh is pierced with fork, about 5 minutes. Watch carefully to be sure quail does not burn.

Serve quail brushed with glaze and accompanied by salad. Garnish with figs and micro greens.

Regina Mehallick
R bistro

R BISTRO
REGINA MEHALLICK, CHEF/
OWNER

888 Massachusetts Avenue
Indianapolis, Indiana 46202

317-423-0312
www.rbistro.com

REGINA MEHALLICK NAVIGATES
her enormous kitchen at R bistro with easy
command. Her diminutive form is relaxed
and efficient, her movements economical and
precise. She says she loves the thrill of cooking
on the line and she thrives on adrenalin, but she
doesn't look like an adrenalin junkie—she looks
like a roguish Mona Lisa.

Her dark brown hair, almost always tucked
under one of her signature scarves, is cropped
to a wavy brown cap to emphasize broad
cheekbones and the huge brown eyes that
glimmer with humor and the pleasure she takes
in her job. Mehallick came late to cooking, and
it's clear she relishes her midlife career change.

At the age of thirty-five, she quit managing medical offices and went to study cooking at Johnson & Wales University in South Carolina, where her husband's job had taken them. Moving again, across the Atlantic this time, she honed her craft in British restaurants and Irish cooking classes.

In her classes at Ballymaloe, in County Cork, all the ingredients they used were fresh: the herbs and lettuces picked straight from the garden; the free-range eggs, chickens, fish and lamb all local. Mehallick was struck by how much better these things tasted, and since for her it is all about taste, she was hooked on the philosophy of using local products.

After returning to the States and moving to Indiana, she decided it was time to open her own place. She was forty-seven years old, and thought, "I'm old enough, and if I don't do it now, I never will. Some things in your life you just need to try."

Finding the right space was difficult (an old castor factory with high brick walls, transformed into a tour de force of chrome, color, and light), but so was finding the sorts of local purveyors she had come to rely on in Ireland and Scotland. Today her food is as fresh and local as she can get it: she buys from local mushroom growers and fish farmers as well as the meat and vegetable producers she has found.

Her cooking is essential and spare, so that the fine ingredients she chooses can shine through. There are no frills or furbelows, no fancy architecture or gimmicks. She cooks meat and fish simply, with oil, salt and pepper, and concentrates on accompaniments to enhance what's on the plate. It is minimalist cooking, with a premium on taste and quality.

At R bistro, the menu of five appetizers, five entrées, and five desserts changes weekly—a tremendous challenge for the kitchen staff. Mehallick is constantly reading, thinking, brainstorming with her chefs, and checking available ingredients for ideas for the menu. She finalizes ideas by Saturday, orders on Monday, gets all the food in on Tuesday, and starts a new menu every Wednesday. By Saturday, they have finally gotten it all down right, and then they change the menu again and start all over.

This extraordinarily ambitious undertaking is possible only because of teamwork. She values her talented staff and recognizes them by name—cooks and servers alike—on her menu, along with the names of the local producers she buys her food from. "Why not credit everyone?" she says. "After all, it's a collaborative effort." That kind of generosity of spirit is reflected throughout the restaurant, and makes dining there a pleasure. You can experience some of the genuine comfort and simplicity of Mehallick's cooking at home with this colorful and warming fall menu.

Butternut Squash Soup

Regina Mehallick, R bistro (Indianapolis)

SOUP

safflower or vegetable oil, as needed

1 onion, chopped

3 stalks celery, chopped

1 leek (white part only), chopped

2 butternut squash, peeled and cut into 1-inch dice

½ to 1 celery root, peeled and diced

1 to 2 teaspoons ground coriander

chicken stock or water, warmed, as needed to cover vegetables

salt and pepper, to taste

heavy whipping cream, as needed

fresh cilantro, chopped, to taste

CROUTE

8 to 12 slices white bread

butter, as needed

4 ounces goat cheese

¼ cup pecans, toasted and chopped

SOUP

Add enough oil to lightly cover the bottom of a large stockpot. Sauté onion over medium heat until translucent. Add celery and leek, stirring to be sure everything is sautéing. Add squash and celery root. Continue to sauté vegetables, not allowing them to brown. Stir in coriander.

When all vegetables are nicely sautéed, add stock or water to cover vegetables. Bring to a boil and then simmer until vegetables are tender. Remove from heat and puree. (Hot soups are most easily pureed with an immersion or hand blender. If pureeing in a countertop blender, cool soup first.)

Strain soup and return to a large, clean pot. Season with salt and pepper. Add cream, starting with 2 tablespoons and adding additional amounts until soup reaches desired consistency. Add cilantro and adjust seasoning.

CROUTE

Cut circles out of bread and sauté in a little butter over medium heat until golden. Drain on paper towel. Top croute with goat cheese and pecans and warm under broiler for a few moments.

Serve soup with croute placed in center of bowl.

Seared Scallops with Sauce Vierge

Regina Mehallick, R bistro (Indianapolis)

9 large scallops (dry, untreated scallops if available)

6 tablespoons olive oil, plus additional for searing scallops

2 tablespoons lemon juice

1 teaspoon coriander seeds, crushed

8 basil leaves, cut into julienne strips

salt and pepper, as needed

2 tomatoes, peeled, seeded and diced

herbs (e.g., tarragon, chives, chervil), for garnish

Slice scallops in half. Place on parchment paper and refrigerate.

Heat a large pan over medium-high heat for scallops. Meanwhile, heat olive oil in a small pan over low to medium-low heat, then add lemon juice. Remove from heat. Add coriander and basil, and infuse the warm oil for a few minutes.

Season scallops with salt and pepper. Place a small amount of olive oil in pan and sear scallops on each side.

Add tomato to sauce. Place a spoonful of sauce on each plate. Top with 3 scallop halves, overlapping and garnished with herbs and topped with a little more sauce.

Pan-Seared Duck Breast with Pomegranate-Nut Sauce, Potato Rösti, and Sautéed Kale

Regina Mehallick, R bistro (Indianapolis)

POTATO RÖSTI

2 large potatoes

salt and pepper, to taste

oil, as needed for cooking rösti

SAUTÉED KALE

1 bunch kale, tough stems removed, chopped

butter, as needed

salt and pepper, to taste

POMEGRANATE-NUT SAUCE

4 tablespoons butter

½ onion, finely chopped

1½ cups walnuts, ground

juice of 4 pomegranates (about 1½ cups)

2 tablespoons fresh lime juice

large pinch of sugar

veal stock reduction, to taste (or substitute reduced chicken broth)

DUCK BREAST

4 duck breasts (5 to 6 ounces each)

salt and pepper, to taste

pomegranate seeds, for garnish

POTATO RÖSTI

Grate potatoes and squeeze in a towel to remove starch. Season with salt and pepper. Form into 4 pancake shapes and cook in oil until golden brown. Keep warm until ready to serve or cool on wire rack, then reheat in oven.

SAUTÉED KALE

Place kale in a large pot and cover with water. Boil until tender, then drain. When ready to sauté, refresh with cold water, draining again and squeezing out excess moisture. Sauté in butter and season with salt and pepper.

POMEGRANATE-NUT SAUCE

Melt butter over medium heat and fry onion until golden. Remove from heat and stir in walnuts. Return to heat, adding pomegranate juice, lime juice, sugar, and veal stock reduction. Cover and simmer gently for 30 minutes or until sauce thickens.

DUCK BREAST

Preheat oven to 400 degrees. Trim duck breasts and score fatty side. Season with salt and pepper. Sear skin side down in a large skillet until crispy, then turn to other side and finish in oven. Cook 3 to 5 minutes. Remove and let rest. Slice before serving.

To serve, place kale near edge of plate with rösti angled against it. Fan sliced duck breast over rösti. Drizzle sauce over duck and onto plate. Garnish with pomegranate seeds.

Pear Sable with Warm Caramel Sauce

Serves 6

Regina Mehallick, R bistro (Indianapolis)

SABLE

1⅓ cups plus 1 tablespoon all-purpose flour
¾ cup powdered sugar
pinch of salt
10 tablespoons (1¼ sticks) unsalted butter
1 egg yolk

PEARS

½ cup plus 1 tablespoon sugar
10 ounces water
juice of ½ lemon
3 pears, peeled, halved, and cored

CARAMEL SAUCE

½ cup plus 1 tablespoon sugar
3 tablespoons water
7 ounces heavy whipping cream
4 tablespoons (½ stick) unsalted butter, cubed
juice of ½ lemon

whipped cream, for garnish
powdered sugar, for garnish

SABLE

Sift or sieve flour and sugar into a medium bowl and add salt. Rub butter and yolk into flour mixture until it comes together, or prepare in food processor, but stop machine as soon as mixture starts coming together. Press mixture together, wrap in plastic wrap, and chill in refrigerator for 30 minutes.

Preheat oven to 300 degrees. Roll out pastry to ¼-inch thickness. Using fluted pastry cutter, stamp out 12 circles 3½ inches in diameter. Place on lined baking sheet. Bake until pale golden color, 15 to 20 minutes.

PEARS

Combine sugar, water, and lemon juice in a medium, stainless steel saucepan and bring to boil. Poach pears in syrup until tender, about 20 minutes. Keep saucepan covered to prevent pears from discoloring. Remove cooked pears from syrup and allow to cool.

CARAMEL SAUCE

Dissolve sugar in water in a small saucepan over low to medium-low heat. Bring to boil and cook, swirling occasionally (do not stir) until mixture caramelizes. Carefully add cream bit by bit until smooth. Remove pot from heat and whisk in cubed butter. When butter is fully incorporated, add lemon juice and stir again. Set aside.

To assemble, place sable on plate and top with a dollop of whipped cream. Slice a pear half into a fan and place on top of cream. Drizzle with caramel sauce and another dollop of cream. Top with another sable and cream. Garnish with caramel sauce and sprinkle with powdered sugar.

David Tallent
Restaurant Tallent

RESTAURANT TALLENT
DAVID TALLENT, CHEF
KRISTEN TALLENT, PASTRY CHEF
AND GENERAL MANAGER

620 West Kirkwood Avenue
Bloomington, Indiana 47404

812-330-9801
www.restauranttallent.com

MENU

• **Two-Color Gazpacho**

• **Pan-Roasted Sea Scallops with Pommes Anna and Chanterelle Mushroom Succotash**

• **Roasted Venison Loin with Creamy Grits and Braised Red Cabbage**

• **Banana Tart**

WHEN DAVE TALLENT TALKS about cooking, and the local ingredients he has discovered, his voice becomes almost reverent, as though he were talking about rare jewels or exotic blooms. The venison from a Martinsville farm, the 10 pounds of fresh asparagus scored from a local farmer, the pancetta he would cure himself, the regional cheeses—found treasures all. His eyes light up, his cheeks turn pinker, his voice gets hushed. The man is in love with food.

Tallent's cooking reflects that love and the influence of his two food heroes: Alice Waters, whose Berkeley restaurant Chez Panisse set the national standard for using seasonal local

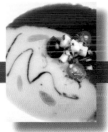

ingredients and Thomas Keller, whose genius and creativity have led many in the food world to declare The French Laundry in northern California the finest restaurant in the U.S. With these two as inspiration, as well as his expert training from the Culinary Institute of America and his own sound food intuitions and skills, he is a formidable force in the kitchen.

Tallent was close to graduating from Indiana University when the lure of the kitchen sent him down a different path. Food had always been an important part of his world, an integral part of family life and celebrations. He'd cooked in a wide range of Bloomington restaurants while he was in school, and realized that cooking had become not just a way to pay the bills but something he actively enjoyed. While working at the Upland brewpub, he met Kristen Britton, fated to become a pastry chef, his wife, and his partner in running Restaurant Tallent. The two got serious about cooking and headed off to study at the CIA (an intense, disciplined, eye-opening experience that Dave says he'd do all over again, just for the fun of it), working in restaurants in New York and Atlanta, before coming back to Bloomington.

Restaurant Tallent is a family affair. Dave is in charge of the kitchen, Kristen designs the dessert menu and runs the front of the house, and Dave's brother Danny is the sous chef. The small kitchen runs with an efficiency and good nature that comes from people who, bound by affection, are on the same wavelength and who don't need to talk much to get things done right.

Tallent's primary commitment in his restaurant is to providing delicious food that highlights the wonderful bounty of southern Indiana. He has an extensive network of local producers, farmers, and artisans from whom he buys as much of the food he serves as possible. An active member of the Slow Food movement and co-leader of Slow Food Bloomington, he puts his money where his mouth is, conducting exhaustive searches for great, organic, local foods. "That's what is in here for me," he says, putting his hand to his heart. "That's what I love."

That commitment is reflected in his frequently changing menu, augmented by nightly specials that showcase mushrooms, ramps, heirloom tomatoes, or whatever happens to be ripe, luscious, and available that week. A constant refrain in Dave's mind as he creates his dishes from these wonderful ingredients is the oft-repeated one-fork test of one of his CIA instructors, who would evaluate the young chefs he taught by taking a single fork and scooping up a bit of everything on the plate. If it doesn't all taste good together, it doesn't work.

Each plate of food at Restaurant Tallent is a masterpiece by the one-fork standard. Get out your fork and test this delectable early fall menu.

Two-Color Gazpacho

Serves 8 to 12 (unstrained) or 4 to 6 (strained)

David Tallent, Restaurant Tallent (Bloomington)

BALSAMIC GLAZE

2 cups balsamic vinegar

SOUP

3 pounds ripe red tomatoes, peeled, seeded, and chopped

3 pounds ripe yellow tomatoes, peeled, seeded, and chopped

1 large cucumber, peeled, seeded, and chopped, divided

1 medium red onion, chopped, divided

1 jalapeño pepper, chopped, divided

1 clove garlic, chopped, divided

4 sprigs thyme, divided

4 sprigs parsley, divided

2 tablespoons red wine vinegar, divided

salt and pepper, to taste

RELISH

2 heirloom tomatoes

½ medium cucumber, cut into ¼-inch dice

¼ red onion, cut into ¼-inch dice

1 small jalapeño pepper, finely minced

salt and pepper, to taste

BALSAMIC GLAZE

Heat balsamic vinegar in a small heavy-bottomed pot at the lowest possible setting for 2 to 3 hours. Do not let the vinegar boil, as it will get bitter and harsh. Reduce to ½ cup.

SOUP

One day before serving, combine red tomatoes and half each of the cucumber, onion, jalapeño, garlic, thyme, and parsley in a large nonreactive bowl. Add 1 tablespoon vinegar and a healthy pinch of salt and pepper; stir to combine. Repeat procedure with yellow tomatoes and remaining soup ingredients. Refrigerate overnight.

RELISH

Quarter tomatoes and remove seeds and juice from middle. Add juice to marinating soups and place both soups in refrigerator overnight. Cut tomatoes into ¼-inch dice and place in a small, nonreactive bowl with cucumber, onion, and jalapeño. Stir to combine and season with salt and pepper. Refrigerate.

The next day, take the soups and relish from the refrigerator. Remove thyme and parsley. Process each soup separately using a food mill, food processor, or blender. Adjust seasonings. For a smoother texture, after processing strain each soup through a fine sieve.

Place soups in individual pitchers or use 2 ladles of the same size. Place each soup in the bowl at same time, 1 on each side. Put spoonful of relish in middle and drops of balsamic glaze around outside edge of soup just before serving.

Pan-Roasted Sea Scallops with Pommes Anna and Chanterelle Mushroom Succotash

David Tallent, Restaurant Tallent (Bloomington)

Pommes Anna

3 medium potatoes

4 tablespoons clarified butter or extra-virgin olive oil, more or less as needed

salt and pepper, to taste

Succotash

¼ cup salt

4 ears corn

1 small zucchini

1 small yellow squash

½ cup shell beans (e.g., fava, lima, cranberry, great northern), cooked or frozen

½ pound chanterelle mushrooms

½ red bell pepper

½ red onion

4 to 5 tablespoons olive oil, divided

salt and pepper, to taste

4 shallots, minced

1 tablespoon (⅛ stick) butter

Scallops

1½ pounds scallops (dry, untreated scallops if available)

3 tablespoons sherry vinegar

salt and pepper, to taste

1 to 3 tablespoons olive oil

Pommes Anna

Preheat oven to 375 degrees. Wash and peel potatoes. Cut to ⅛-inch thick using mandoline or sharp knife. Hold slices in water.

Dry potatoes well with a towel. Brush a nonstick pan or silicone baking sheet with clarified butter or olive oil. Arrange potatoes in 6 individual circles, overlapping slices in each circle. Drizzle each circle with butter or oil.

Place potatoes in oven for about 30 to 35 minutes. When browned and crispy, pull them out and season with salt and pepper. Hold on a paper towel–lined plate in a warm place.

Succotash

Boil a large pot of water with ¼ cup of salt. Drop corn in water for about 4 minutes. Remove and place on plate. Let cool for 10 minutes, then cut corn off cob. (Reserve cobs for soup, stock, or sauce.) Drop zucchini and yellow squash in the water for about 3 minutes. Remove and plunge into ice water until cool. If using frozen beans, drop them in the boiling water for 3 to 4 minutes, then place in ice water.

Clean mushrooms with damp cloth or pastry brush. Slice medium and large mushrooms in half. Dice red bell pepper, onion, zucchini, and yellow squash about size of corn kernels. Hold each separately.

Heat a large sauté pan over medium to medium-high heat and add 2 tablespoons of olive oil. Add mushrooms, and let sit for 3 minutes. Stir and let sit for 3 more minutes. If pan looks dry, add another tablespoon olive oil. After another minute or so, salt and pepper mushrooms and add shallots. Cook until shallots are translucent. Drain on paper towel-lined plate. Separate chanterelles and shallots and set aside.

Heat a large sauté pan over medium to medium-high heat and add 2 tablespoons olive oil. Sauté onions for 3 minutes with salt and pepper. Add red bell pepper and a little more salt and pepper, and cook for 3 more minutes. Add corn and cook 2 more minutes. Add zucchini, yellow squash, and beans and cook for about 4 more minutes. Season with salt and pepper and add butter and chanterelles; cook until warm.

SCALLOPS

Dry scallops with a towel, while heating a large sauté pan over medium to medium-high heat. Add 1 tablespoon olive oil, then place the scallops in the pan, being careful not to overcrowd. Cook for 5 to 6 minutes, and then turn and cook for 2 to 5 minutes more, depending on desired doneness. Remove scallops from pan and keep warm. Repeat with remaining scallops, as needed.

Add sherry vinegar and reserved shallots to the cooking juices in hot pan. Cook for 3 minutes. Add salt and pepper and whisk in enough of the remaining olive oil to create sauce.

To serve, place one circle of pommes Anna on a warm plate and arrange scallops on top of the potatoes. Spoon some of the succotash over the top, and finish with a tablespoon of pan sauce.

[103]

Roasted Venison Loin with Creamy Grits and Braised Red Cabbage

David Tallent, Restaurant Tallent (Bloomington)

Serves 6

CREAMY GRITS

2 cups Wib's Stone Ground Grits (see Sources)

12½ cups water, divided

2½ teaspoons salt

6 tablespoons (¾ stick) butter

salt and pepper, to taste

BRAISED RED CABBAGE

½ large head red cabbage

1 Granny Smith apple

½ red onion

2 tablespoons butter, or as needed

1 cups red wine vinegar

1 cup apple cider

2 cups chicken stock or broth

½ sprig rosemary

½ sprig thyme

1 stem parsley

½ bay leaf

2 peppercorns

2 juniper berries

VENISON LOIN

1 tablespoon olive oil, or more as needed

2½ to 3 pounds Double-T Ranch venison tenderloin (see Sources), divided into 6 equal portions

salt and pepper, to taste

½ shallot, minced

½ sprig rosemary

½ sprig thyme

1 stem parsley

½ bay leaf

2 peppercorns

2 juniper berries

½ cup zinfandel

½ cup chicken stock

1 tablespoon butter, cold

CREAMY GRITS

Cover grits with 6 cups water in large bowl and stir for several minutes. Drain in a fine mesh strainer. Put remaining water and salt in a 3-quart, heavy-bottomed casserole and dissolve salt over medium heat. Whisk in grits in a fine stream so that no lumps form.

Gradually increase temperature to 180 degrees and hold it there for 20 minutes. Mixture will remain separated; stir every 2 to 3 minutes to prevent sticking. When water is absorbed, stir every 15 minutes, scraping down sides and bottom. Cook for 2½ to 3 hours. When done, stir in 6 tablespoons butter. Keep warm, covered with plastic wrap.

Braised Red Cabbage

Peel off outer leaves from a half head of cabbage and slice in half again. Slice into thin shreds; wash and reserve. Thinly slice apple (leaving skin on) and onion.

Warm butter in a large casserole or wide pot over low to medium heat. Add onions and sweat for 3 minutes. Add apples and cabbage and cook for 6 minutes, stirring often. Add vinegar and cider and let reduce by half, then add stock and reduce by one-fourth.

In cheesecloth or coffee filter, tie up herbs and spices and place in pot. Cook 10 minutes or until cabbage is soft and liquid reduces to glaze on cabbage. Remove herbs and spices and discard.

Venison Loin

Heat a large skillet over medium-high heat. Add 1 tablespoon olive oil. When oil shimmers, salt and pepper venison well. Waiting 45 seconds between each addition to allow pan to recover heat, place 3 pieces of venison in pan. Cook meat on one side for 3 minutes, then roll a little and cook 3 more minutes, until all sides are seared. Repeat with remaining pieces, adding oil to the pan as needed.

At this point the meat should be rare. To bring it to medium-rare, place in 350-degree oven for about 4 minutes; add 2 to 3 minutes for each additional degree of doneness. (Note: Venison cooked beyond medium may be dry and chewy.) When meat is done, set on plate in warm place to rest.

Return the pan to stovetop; over medium

heat add shallots, herbs, spices, and wine and reduce by three-fourths. Add chicken stock and reduce by half. Be sure to scrape the browned bits off the bottom of the pan. When properly reduced, sauce should almost coat the back of the spoon. Add butter over high heat, whisking vigorously. Adjust salt and pepper and strain through fine sieve.

To serve, slice venison against grain into 4 or 5 slices and arrange on plate with cabbage and grits. Cover with sauce.

Banana Tart

Kristen Tallent, Restaurant Tallent (Bloomington)

Tart Dough

22 tablespoons (2¾ sticks) butter, at room temperature

¾ cup sugar

1 egg

¼ teaspoon lemon juice

3¼ cups flour, sifted

Nut Filling

12 tablespoons (1½ sticks) butter, at room temperature

¼ cup sugar

2 eggs

1 teaspoon vanilla extract

1 teaspoon almond extract

10 ounces ground pecans

½ cup flour, sifted

4 to 6 bananas

sugar, as needed

butter pecan ice cream

Tart Dough

Combine butter and sugar in the bowl of electric mixer. Cream until mixture is pale yellow and sugar has dissolved. Add egg and lemon juice. Add sifted flour, mixing until flour is just combined. Chill dough in refrigerator for at least 35 to 40 minutes.

Nut Filling

Cream together butter and sugar until mixture is pale yellow and sugar has dissolved. Add eggs, extracts, pecans, and sifted flour. Mix until just combined.

Roll out chilled tart dough to ⅙- to ¼-inch thickness. Using a knife, cut out circles of dough large enough to cover the insides of 12 4-inch tart shells. Place dough in tart shells, settling it in with your fingers and cutting off any excess dough hanging over sides. Place tart shells in freezer for 20 minutes. Meanwhile, preheat oven to 350 degrees.

Fill the chilled tart shells with nut filling to just below the edge of tart dough. Bake tarts for 25 to 30 minutes, or until filling is golden brown and completely set. Let tarts cool until they can be removed from tart shells.

Before serving, cut bananas diagonally into ¼-inch slices. Arrange slices in concentric circles on top of filling, and cover with thin layer of sugar. Using a kitchen torch or oven broiler, caramelize sugar on top of the bananas. The sugar should be golden brown, but not burnt.

Serve with your favorite ice cream. Restaurant Tallent recommends butter pecan.

John "Peach" Gettelfinger

RockWall Bistro

ROCKWALL BISTRO

John "Peach" Gettelfinger,
Chef

Guy and Joni Sillings,
Owners

3426 Paoli Pike
Floyds Knobs, Indiana 47119

812-948-1705
www.rockwallbistro.com

MENU

• **Cream of Asparagus Soup**

• **Wilted Green Salad with Goat Cheese and Walnut Vinaigrette**

• **Shrimp Brochette with Roasted Corn Salsa**

• **Bad Elmer's New York Strip**

JOHN GETTELFINGER IS A SOLID GUY
with bristly short hair who looks like he gets his
own way a lot, so it's kind of endearing that he
answers to the name "Peach" and says his all-time
favorite meal is his grandmother's chicken and
dumplings.

Peach got involved in the restaurant business
when he began washing dishes to earn money
as an undergraduate at Ball State University.
He hated dishwashing, but loved the restaurant
culture, the excitement when things got busy and

the satisfaction the chefs felt when they put out a product they were really proud of. He got a job in the kitchen at Foxfire's—now, regrettably, an IHOP—and started to learn from Chef Tony Huelster. "Chef Tony was really open to teaching people who wanted to learn, and I was always underfoot," he says. He came in early and stayed late, figuring that it was a free education he should take advantage of. He learned fast, cooking on the line and then progressing to sous chef. It became clear to him that cooking was what he wanted to do, and he stayed at Foxfire's for three-and-a-half years.

When Chef Tony took off to run his own place (Bonge's Tavern in Perkinsville), Peach followed, and worked as the sous chef there for more than three years. It was only the desire to move home to New Albany that persuaded him to leave and come down to the RockWall Bistro where he was sous chef and then executive chef.

The RockWall Bistro is built right into the wall of an actual limestone quarry. Owned by Guy and Joni Sillings, the restaurant is a converted cottage. The patio is sheltered on one side by the rock wall, with a waterfall trickling down its side, giving it a grotto-like effect; twinkling lights are strung across the ceiling. With items like fried green tomatoes with Cajun aïoli, wilted green salad with goat cheese, and fried rock game hen, the menu is traditional American with a Southern twist.

Peach's thinking about food begins with the idea that "you take what you've got and let it stand on its own." He doesn't believe in adding excessive ingredients to a plate so that the essential nature of the food is lost. Increasingly he is grounding his own cooking style in traditional ethnic cuisines like Italian and Asian, and he is gaining a new appreciation for Southern cooking, a necessity when he moved back to southern Indiana.

For him, the excitement of cooking comes in the creative process, when you have imagined a dish and get that it is working—when you see it or taste it and know that you are on the right track. It all comes together when he walks through the dining room and people he doesn't know grab him and tell him the food is great.

Influenced by his Bonge's days, he sees himself eventually having his own small restaurant, with a limited number of appetizers and entrées, only a couple of desserts, and a menu he can change seasonally—even monthly—to showcase what's fresh and local. When that happens, look for delicious recipes like the ones on this Indiana summer menu.

Cream of Asparagus Soup

John Gettelfinger, RockWall Bistro (Floyds Knobs)

2 bunches pencil-thin asparagus, chopped, tips reserved

1 small onion, chopped

4 tablespoons butter

5 tablespoons flour

4 cups whole milk

¼ teaspoon saffron threads

1 tablespoon salt

½ teaspoon white pepper

In a medium saucepan sauté asparagus and onion in butter over medium heat until tender. Add flour and cook until the flour loses its raw smell and has a nutty aroma. Add milk, saffron, salt, and pepper, stirring constantly to prevent scorching.

When the soup is thickened, puree. (Hot soups are most easily pureed with an immersion or hand blender. If pureeing in a countertop blender, cool soup first.) Return pot of soup to stovetop and add asparagus tips. Simmer for 5 minutes, then serve.

Wilted Green Salad with Goat Cheese and Walnut Vinaigrette

John Gettelfinger, RockWall Bistro (Floyds Knobs)

WALNUT VINAIGRETTE

2 tablespoons minced shallots

2 tablespoons chopped toasted walnuts

1½ teaspoons salt

1 teaspoon sugar

¼ cup sherry vinegar

¾ cup olive oil

SALAD

1 bunch collard greens, washed and stemmed

1 bunch mustard greens, washed and stemmed

1 bunch turnip greens, washed and stemmed

½ teaspoon salt

¼ cup apple cider vinegar

1 tablespoon butter

4 ounces Capriole goat cheese (see Sources), crumbled

red bell pepper, finely diced, to taste

freshly ground black pepper, to taste

WALNUT VINAIGRETTE

In a small mixing bowl, combine shallots, walnuts, salt, sugar, and vinegar. Slowly whisk in olive oil until incorporated. Set aside.

SALAD

Place greens in a large stockpot with salt and vinegar. Add enough water to cover greens. Bring to boil, then reduce heat and simmer for 40 minutes. Drain greens in colander.

In a large sauté pan, brown butter and add greens. When heated through, place in large bowl. Top with goat cheese, red bell pepper, and vinaigrette. Finish with black pepper.

Shrimp Brochette with Roasted Corn Salsa

John Gettelfinger, RockWall Bistro (Floyds Knobs)

SALSA

1 ear fresh sweet corn, shucked and washed

1 red bell pepper

¼ teaspoon minced jalapeño pepper

2 tablespoons minced red onion

salt and pepper, to taste

SHRIMP BROCHETTE

1 clove garlic, minced

1 tablespoon olive oil

1 tablespoon lime juice

¼ teaspoon salt

¼ teaspoon pepper

20 large shrimp, peeled and deveined

bamboo skewers

SALSA

Preheat oven to 350 degrees. Place corn and red bell pepper in oven and roast until pepper skin is blistered. Remove both, placing red bell pepper in zip-top plastic bag. When pepper has cooled, peel, seed, and dice. When corn has cooled, cut kernels off cob. Combine red bell pepper, corn, jalapeño, and onion. Season with salt and pepper and refrigerate.

SHRIMP BROCHETTE

Soak 4 10-inch bamboo skewers in warm water for about 15 minutes. Combine garlic, olive oil, lime juice, salt, and pepper in large mixing bowl and toss with shrimp. Let sit for 30 minutes.

Light grill and bring to high heat. Skewer shrimp and grill about 2 minutes per side.

Portion salsa on plates and top with shrimp brochette.

Bad Elmer's New York Strip

John Gettelfinger, RockWall Bistro (Floyds Knobs)

12 ounces Upland Brewing Company Bad
    Elmer's Porter (see Sources)

4 strips bacon, diced

3 tablespoons flour

½ cup pearl onions, peeled

½ cup button mushrooms, quartered

6 ounces strong beef stock

4 10-ounce New York strip steaks

salt and pepper, to taste

In a small saucepan over medium heat, reduce beer by half. In a medium saucepan cook bacon over medium heat until crisp, then sprinkle with flour. Stirring constantly, add onions, mushrooms, beef stock, and reduced beer. Continue stirring until sauce is thick and onions are tender. Season to taste with salt and pepper.

Light grill and bring to high heat. Season steaks with salt and pepper, and grill to desired temperature. Serve grilled steaks topped with warm sauce.

Josh Lashlee
Three Market Street

THREE MARKET STREET
Josh Lashlee, Chef &
Proprietor

*3 Market Street
Newburgh, Indiana 47630*

812-490-6990

MENU

• **Succotash Soup (Fava Bean Puree with Corn and Fennel Relish and Seared Diver Scallop)**

• **Alice's Summer Salad**

• **Pistachio- and Carmelized Shallot–Crusted Rack of Lamb with Summer Bean "Cassoulet"**

• **Lemon Soufflé**

JOSH LASHLEE, AT TWENTY-FIVE, is young to have his own restaurant, but his intensity and his steady, dark-browed gaze belie his youth. His face may lighten with a smile as he talks about his calling and his restaurant, but it is tempered with the knowledge that life can be a serious business. His is an intellectual, thoughtful approach to food, and if he is driven by a joyful passion as well, he keeps that hidden from the casual observer.

If Plato were writing this cookbook, he might well peg Lashlee as a "philosopher chef." "Life is easier and more satisfying if you do the things you

are good at," Lashlee says, explaining why he chose to follow a culinary career rather than complete the few remaining credits of his history degree (something he still plans to do one day). He echoes that idea again later, saying that people (read customers) will have a better experience if they let experts (here, chefs) do what they do best.

For Lashlee, the path to expert cooking led from Bowling Green, Kentucky, to Nashville, Tennessee, where he learned classical techniques at Arthur's in Union Station and the Wild Boar, and then to Evansville, his fiancée's hometown, where he was first sous chef, then chef for four years at Lorenzo's.

Opening his own restaurant was the next logical step for him, backed by encouraging customers who wanted to see him in his own place. The building at 3 Market Street—just a block off the river in Newburgh, Indiana—was available, and though the economy was slow in 2003, he took the plunge.

Cooking comes naturally and easily to Lashlee, if running the business end of things remains something of a less enjoyable challenge. He looks at every dish as a complete whole—something greater than the sum of its individual ingredients. Different things work together for a reason, he says more than once: some things are meant to come together on a plate; others are not.

Thus, many cuisines end up with variations on common themes; at some level, jambalaya is paella, after all. It's all what a particular culture does with indigenous ingredients. He sums up his thinking about food this way—"take the freshest and best ingredients there are and do little to them—that's the key." Good food will stay good if you don't tamper with it too much.

But food is about more than just taste; it is about intangibles as well. Lashlee notes that you can have an amazing sensory experience at a restaurant like Charlie Trotter's, but home cooking is where you taste your own history. This reinforces his view that fancier is by no means always better.

Lashlee loves to cook with local products when availability and cost make it possible. He builds a new dish around an ingredient he has on hand, or finds in the market, often thinking through a new dish while in the throes of insomnia. He loves working with fish—when you cook with beef, he says, it is bound to be beefy, but fish can be a palette for many flavors—and he is sensitive to which foods taste right at different times of the year. Lamb goes with spring, for instance, game with fall. This late spring/early summer menu, with its seafood, lamb, and seasonal vegetables, perfectly illustrates the cooking philosophy of this thoughtful young chef.

Succotash Soup (Fava Bean Puree with Corn and Fennel Relish and Seared Diver Scallop)

Josh Lashlee, Three Market Street (Newburgh)

Soup

1½ cups frozen fava beans (available in Asian markets)

1½ cups chicken stock

1 cup heavy whipping cream

salt and white pepper, to taste

Relish

1 small fennel bulb

1 tablespoon oil

1 ear fresh corn, cut off cob

1 teaspoon Cajun seasoning (e.g., Paul Prudhomme's Blackened Redfish Magic)

Scallops

4 medium diver scallops (dry, untreated scallops if available)

1 teaspoon oil

salt and pepper, to taste

Soup

Thaw and peel fava beans. Simmer in chicken stock 30 minutes, or until tender. Puree soup. (Hot soups are most easily pureed with an immersion or hand blender. If pureeing in a countertop blender, cool soup first.) Return the soup to the stovetop and reheat with cream, salt, and white pepper. Do not boil.

Relish

Slice fennel bulb into julienne strips, removing core. Heat oil over medium-low heat and sweat fennel, covered, for 20 minutes or until translucent and nearly tender, being careful not to let it burn. Add corn and Cajun seasoning and cook for 5 more minutes.

Scallops

Just before serving, heat oil to very hot in a small skillet, pat scallops dry on paper towels, and season with salt and pepper. Sear for 2 minutes on each side.

Ladle 8 ounces soup each into 4 wide bowls. Top with a portion of relish and a seared scallop.

Alice's Summer Salad

Josh Lashlee, Three Market Street (Newburgh)

4 cups loosely packed
  mesclun greens
1 small red bell pepper,
  chopped
1 small yellow bell pepper,
  chopped
½ cup fresh blueberries
¼ cup shelled pistachios
Ma Knapp's salad dressing
  (recipe below)

Divide mesclun greens among 4 salad plates. Top with peppers, blueberries, and pistachios. Drizzle each salad with 2 tablespoons Ma Knapp's salad dressing.

Ma Knapp's Salad Dressing

1 teaspoon Dijon mustard
⅓ cup apple cider vinegar
2 tablespoons water
⅓ cup sugar
¼ cup salad oil
2 teaspoons grated onion
salt and pepper, to taste

Whisk together mustard and vinegar in small bowl. Add water, sugar, and oil, whisking thoroughly. Add onion and season with salt and pepper. Stir well before serving.

Pistachio- and Carmelized Shallot–Crusted Rack of Lamb with Summer Bean "Cassoulet"

Serves 4

Josh Lashlee, Three Market Street (Newburgh)

LAMB

3 tablespoons oil, divided

2 tablespoons finely chopped shallots

2 tablespoons ground pistachios

¼ cup panko (Japanese-style breadcrumbs; available in Asian markets)

1 tablespoon honey

pinch finely chopped fresh thyme

salt and pepper, to taste

4 12-ounce whole racks of baby lamb (preferably New Zealand)

2 tablespoons Dijon mustard

CASSOULET

1 tablespoon butter

2 tablespoons chopped onion

¼ cup each baby green beans, wax beans, peeled fresh fava beans, and legume sprouts (or equivalent mixture of fresh, in-season beans or peas)

½ cup chicken stock

salt and pepper, to taste

¼ cup chopped fresh tomato

1 tablespoon chopped fresh basil

chopped parsley, to taste

thyme sprigs, for garnish

LAMB

Preheat oven to 400 degrees. Heat 1 tablespoon oil in a small saucepan and slowly brown shallots over medium heat, stirring occasionally, for 15 minutes or until soft and golden. Remove from heat and add pistachios, panko, honey, and thyme, stirring well. Season with salt and pepper.

Heat remaining oil to very hot in a large, heavy skillet. Season lamb racks with salt and pepper and quickly sear on all sides. Remove lamb from the skillet and spread the top of each rack with ½ tablespoon Dijon mustard. Press one-fourth of crust mixture evenly over each rack.

Finish in oven until desired temperature is reached—130 degrees for rare, 145 degrees for medium, 160 degrees for well-done. Remove from oven and let rest for at least 3 minutes before slicing.

CASSOULET

Melt butter in a medium skillet and sweat onion over medium-low heat until translucent but not brown. Add bean mixture and cook for 3 minutes to heat through. Add chicken stock and cook, uncovered, for 5 minutes, seasoning with salt and pepper. Just before serving, remove from heat and stir in tomato and basil.

To serve, divide cassoulet among 4 plates. Cut each lamb rack into 4 double-thickness chops and arrange over cassoulet. Sprinkle with chopped parsley and garnish with thyme sprigs.

Lemon Soufflé

Serves 4

Josh Lashlee, Three Market Street (Newburgh)

8 tablespoons (1 stick) unsalted butter, plus additional for greasing ramekins

¾ cup sugar, plus additional for ramekins

½ cup fresh lemon juice

2½ teaspoons finely minced lemon peel

4 large eggs, separated

Butter 4 8-ounce ramekins; dust with sugar. Melt 8 tablespoons butter in a heavy medium saucepan over medium-low heat. Add sugar and stir until mixture is opaque, about 2 minutes. Stir in lemon juice and lemon peel. Whisk in egg yolks. Cook over medium-low heat until mixture thickens and reaches 180 degrees, whisking constantly, about 12 minutes. Do not boil. Transfer mixture to a large bowl and cool to room temperature, about 30 minutes.

Position rack in center of oven and preheat to 400 degrees. Using an electric mixer, beat egg whites in another large bowl until stiff but not dry. Fold one-fourth of the beaten egg whites into lemon mixture to lighten. Fold remaining egg whites into lemon mixture.

Divide soufflé mixture among prepared ramekins. Place filled ramekins in a large roasting pan. Fill the pan with enough hot water to come halfway up sides of ramekins. Bake soufflés until golden brown on top, about 14 minutes.

Using tongs, remove soufflés from the water and serve immediately.

Martin Frannea
Truffles

TRUFFLES
MARTIN FRANNEA, EXECUTIVE CHEF
MARK KIANG, OWNER

1131 South College Mall Road
Bloomington, Indiana 47401

812-330-1111

MENU

• **Spinach Salad with Roasted Corn, Queso Fresco, and Avocado with Red Chile and Mango Vinaigrette**

• **Pear-Shaped Potato Croquettes with Black Truffle Butter**

• **Five-Peppercorn Roasted Squab with White Port Reduction**

• **Apple Crepias with Tahitian Vanilla Sauce**

MARTIN FRANNEA IS A STUDY IN contrasts—a serious man who can look pretty forbidding when he is listening to something he thinks is silly, but who can also kick back and laugh heartily when he is talking about the things he enjoys. Food is undoubtedly one of those things.

Frannea has unambiguous opinions on the subject. He scorns what he calls "neat-o food," food chefs cook primarily to impress their peers, and he doesn't think much of the show-business

styles of celebrity chefs, who he thinks are forced to make compromises in their work. His food philosophy is simple: "Until you are Charlie Trotter, you need to be making food that is yummy."

And yummy his food is. Although it is often beautiful, it is not avant-garde, or architecturally elaborate, or filled with wildly exotic ingredients. Rather, it is focused on what he thinks his customers want to eat. Most of his recipe ideas come to him not in the kitchen but in the shower, while his mind is still fresh and caffeine-free.

He focuses on innovative American fare that shows more than a hint of his Southwestern roots. No matter how his menu changes, though, there is always a variation of Frannea's favorite invention: seared duck breast with a vanilla-rum sauce, served with a potato croquette stuffed with black truffle butter.

Frannea's real passion is for sweets, however, and when he lets his inner pastry chef loose he spends hours handcrafting chocolates and other gorgeous desserts. Especially good are a layered confection of shortbread, chantilly cream, and fresh berries; and a divine dark-chocolate crème brûlée.

Cooking was not Frannea's first career choice. Growing up in Austin, Texas, young Martin had cooked for his family since the age of nine and cultivated his passion for food on twice-yearly trips to exotic places with his Norway-based father. Nonetheless, he went after a degree in Fine Arts, and started a sculpture studio. It was the lure of a regular paycheck that led to his discovery that he could parlay his fascination with food and art into a career. In 1994 he enrolled in the Culinary Institute of America to train as a chef; two years later he was back in Austin as chef at Zoot.

By the time Mark Kiang, the owner of Bloomington's Truffles, found his résumé on the Internet, Frannea was burned out from three years of high-intensity work and ready to give up on the hot Texas summers. Kiang flew down to Austin to meet him and studied his menus, finding a cosmopolitan style that was not too far-fetched for Bloomington and an authenticity that he wanted for his restaurant. He hired him and Truffles opened soon after, in December 2001.

The interior of the restaurant is at once sophisticated and tranquil. The 56° Bar (named for the proper temperature to cellar wine) has high red walls, lots of wood panels, and black accents. The dining room itself has white walls, white linens, and tables far enough apart to give a sense of ordered space and quiet. It is a classy backdrop in which to enjoy Frannea's creative cuisine, such as the early fall menu he shares with us here.

Spinach Salad with Roasted Corn, Queso Fresco, and Avocado with Red Chile and Mango Vinaigrette

Serves 6

Martin Frannea, Truffles (Bloomington)

ROASTED CORN

2 cups fresh yellow corn kernels

1 tablespoon olive oil, pomace olive oil, or vegetable oil

VINAIGRETTE

1 large fresh mango, peeled and diced

juice of 2 limes

¼ cup Sriracha (Thai red chile sauce)

½ cup water

pinch of kosher salt, plus additional to taste

pinch of ground black pepper, plus additional to taste

olive oil, as needed

SALAD

½ pound spinach or greens, washed and dried

2 Hass avocados

4 small tomatoes, sliced

1 cup queso fresco, crumbled

ROASTED CORN

Preheat oven to 300 degrees. Mix corn with oil and spread out on sheet pan. Bake until kernels brown slightly, at least 1 hour. Allow corn to cool, and dab with paper towel to soak up excess oil. Set aside.

VINAIGRETTE

Place mango, lime juice, Sriracha, water, and pinch of salt and pepper in blender. Puree until smooth. With blender running on high speed, slowly drizzle in oil until vinaigrette thickens somewhat. Adjust seasoning.

SALAD

Arrange spinach in tall mound on each chilled salad plate. Peel and slice avocados, and adorn plates with avocado slices. Sprinkle roasted corn, tomato, and cheese on top of spinach. Spoon on vinaigrette just before serving.

Pear-Shaped Potato Croquettes with Black Truffle Butter

Martin Frannea, Truffles (Bloomington)

12 tablespoons (1½ sticks) butter, divided

½ ounce black truffle peelings (or substitute 4 tablespoons truffle butter for peelings and decrease butter to 8 tablespoons)

3 pounds large russet or Yukon Gold potatoes

kosher salt, to taste, divided

8 egg yolks

2 cups all-purpose flour

ground black pepper, to taste

1 quart whole milk

4 eggs, lightly beaten

6 cups panko (Japanese-style breadcrumbs; available in Asian markets)

vegetable oil, as needed for deep-frying (or ½ cup vegetable oil, if baking croquettes)

If not using packaged truffle butter, mix black truffle peelings into 4 tablespoons of softened, creamed butter. Chill truffle butter until hard.

Peel and cut each potato into 8 to 10 equal-sized pieces. Place potatoes and salt in cold water. Boil until potatoes are just tender. Drain well. Let potatoes steam dry in warm place for 10 minutes.

Pass potatoes and 8 tablespoons butter through a food mill or potato ricer. Salt to taste. Fold in egg yolks until just blended; do not overwork. Spread this mixture onto a sheet pan. Wrap loosely with plastic film and chill for 2 hours.

Shape cooled mixture into 8 equal balls. Divide truffle butter into 8 equal portions and insert into the center of each ball. Form each ball into a pear shape and chill for 1 hour on sheet pan.

Season flour with pepper. Combine milk and eggs. Bread the croquettes by dredging in seasoned flour; shake off any excess. Dip in egg wash to coat fully. Coat with breadcrumbs, shaking off any excess.

Deep-fry at 350 degrees or brush with ½ cup vegetable oil and bake in 350-degree oven until golden brown.

Five-Peppercorn Roasted Squab with White Port Reduction

Serves 8

Martin Frannea, Truffles (Bloomington)

½ bottle (1½ cups) white port

8 whole squab (or substitute whole quail or duck breast)

olive oil, as needed

kosher salt, to taste

white peppercorns, ground, to taste

black peppercorns, ground, to taste

green peppercorns, ground, to taste

pink peppercorns, ground, to taste

Szechuan peppercorns, ground, to taste (if available)

8 tablespoons (1 stick) butter, cold and cubed

chopped chives

Bring white port to boil, then lower to simmer. Reduce to ½ cup.

Preheat oven to 400 degrees. Remove any giblets from the squab and remove the first joint of the wing bones from each bird. Rub each bird inside and out with olive oil, salt, and peppercorn mixture.

Heat ⅛ inch of oil to smoking point in a large skillet and lightly brown the breast side of each bird. Place squab on wire rack on top of sheet pan. Roast birds in oven until they reach desired doneness (an internal temperature of 140 to 150 degrees).

Remove squab from oven and let rest in a warm place while finishing the sauce. Bring port reduction to a boil and turn off burner. Whisk in butter until the sauce emulsifies to desired thickness. Season with salt, pepper, and chives and serve with squab.

Apple Crepias with Tahitian Vanilla Sauce

Serves 8

Martin Frannea, Truffles (Bloomington)

VANILLA SAUCE
2 cups heavy whipping cream
2 cups whole milk
2 Tahitian vanilla beans
10 egg yolks
1 cup sugar
pinch of salt
1 ounce dark rum, optional

APPLE CREPIAS
2 sheets frozen puff pastry
3 eggs, beaten
7 Granny Smith apples, peeled and cored
sugar, to taste

powdered sugar, for dusting
1 pint fresh berries, for garnish
mint sprigs, for garnish

VANILLA SAUCE
Place cream and milk in a medium saucepan. Cut vanilla beans in half lengthwise and scrape the seeds from the insides with a dull knife. Add seeds and pods to saucepan. Bring this mixture to a boil and remove from heat; let steep 1 hour.

Bring the cream mixture back to a boil and remove from heat again. Place egg yolks in a mixing bowl and whisk in sugar and salt. Slowly whisk one-third of the hot cream mixture into egg yolks, then add remainder of cream mixture and mix well.

Return mixture to the saucepan and place over high heat. Run a rubber spatula along the bottom of pan in a figure-eight pattern continuously until sauce reaches 184 degrees.

Immediately pour vanilla sauce through a fine sieve into a metal container and place in an ice bath. Stir sauce occasionally until cold. Stir in rum, if desired, and set aside.

APPLE CREPIAS
Preheat oven to 350 degrees. Brush each sheet of puff pastry liberally with egg wash, cut into 6- to 8-inch circles and place on a parchment paper–lined cookie sheet. Chill.

Slice apples ⅛-inch thick on mandoline or with a sharp knife. Arrange slices in an overlapping spiral pattern on each pastry circle, making sure to leave ½-inch border all the way around. Brush tops with remaining egg wash and dust with generous amount of sugar.

Bake, rotating trays after 7 minutes, until edges of apple slices begin to brown.

Dust each of the crepias with powdered sugar and serve immediately in a pool of vanilla sauce. Garnish with berries and mint.

Restaurant Locations

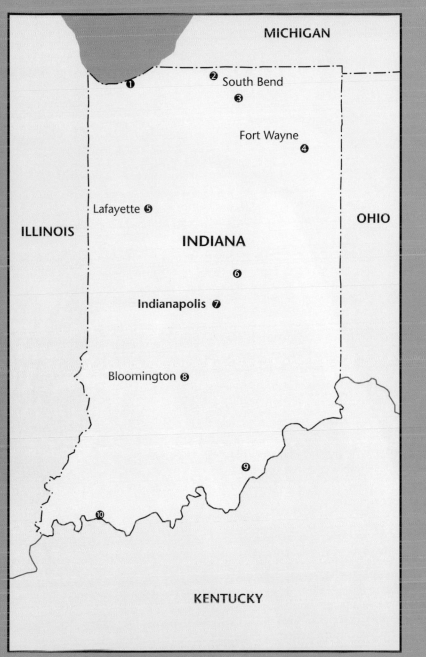

❶ Miller Bakery Café
555 Lake Street
Gary, IN 46403

❷ LaSalle Grill
115 West Colfax Avenue
South Bend, IN 46601

❸ Citrus at the Checkerberry Inn
62644 County Road 37
Goshen, IN 46528

❹ Joseph Decuis
191 North Main Street
Roanoke, IN 46783

❺ Maize, An American Grill
112 North 3rd Street
Lafayette, IN 47901

❻ Bonge's Tavern
9830 West 280 North
Perkinsville, IN 46011

❼ Oakleys Bistro
1464 West 86th Street
Indianapolis, IN 46260

Elements
415 North Alabama Street
Indianapolis, IN 46204

R bistro
888 Massachusetts Avenue
Indianapolis, IN 46202

Dunaway's Palazzo Ossigeno
351 South East Street
Indianapolis, IN 46204

❽ Restaurant Tallent
620 West Kirkwood Avenue
Bloomington, IN 47404

Truffles
1131 South College Mall Road
Bloomington, IN 47401

Limestone Grille
2920 East Covenanter Drive
Bloomington, IN 47401

❾ RockWall Bistro
3426 Paoli Pike
Floyds Knobs, IN 47119

❿ Three Market Street
3 Market Street
Newburgh, IN 47630

The chefs in this book rely on many fine Indiana farmers and producers. Here is just a sampling of what Indiana farms have to offer.

Sources

Capriole Farms

Goat cheese
JUDY SCHAD
P.O. Box 117
10329 Newcut Road
Greenville, IN 47124
812-923-9408
caprioleinc@aol.com
www.capriolegoatcheese.com

County Line Orchards

Apples, peaches, pears
DAVID DOUD
7877 West 400 North
Wabash, IN 46992
765-833-6122
doudone@netusa1.net

Deer Heart Woods

Vegetables and herbs
AMY COUNTRYMAN
Bloomington, IN
812-339-4410

Double T Ranch

Farm-raised venison
TIM TAGUE
2913 Hollow Branch Trail
Martinsville, IN 46151
888-349-1889
doubletranch@hotmail.com
www.venisondeerfarmer.com

Fungus Among Us

Oyster and shiitake mushrooms
MARCIA WILSON
9255 E. 106th Street
Fishers, IN 46038
317-603-5566
wanderw@iquest.net

Great Circle Farm

BETH NEFF AND ZELDA STOLTZFUS
201 North 22nd Street
Goshen, IN 46526
574-533-7936
zebe2@juno.com

Harvest Moon Flower Farm

Flowers, fruit, vegetables, herbs
LINDA CHAPMAN AND DERYL DALE
P.O. Box 435
Route 1
Spencer, IN 47460
812-829-3517
www.harvestmoonflowerfarm.com

Heartland Family Farm

Organic fruits and vegetables
TERESA BIRTLES
Bedford, IN
812-797-6274

Hickoryworks
Shagbark hickory syrup
GORDON JONES AND SHERRIE YARLING
3615 Peoga Road
Trafalgar, IN 46181-9649
317-878-5648
syrup@iquest.net
www.hickoryworks.com

Meadowlark Farms
Fresh Indiana produce
MARCIA VELDMAN
Bloomington, IN
812-988-4956

Poe Stock Farm
Pasture-raised lamb
STANLEY POE
2213 W. State Road 144
Franklin, IN 46131
317-738-0863
poehamps@yahoo.com

Red Gold
Canned tomato products
P.O. Box 83
Elwood, IN 46036
765-754-7527
www.redgold.com

Red Rosa Farm
Fresh vegetables and herbs
CATHY CROSSON
Route 1, Box 596
Spencer, IN 47460
812-829-4016

The Swiss Connection
Cheese, ice cream, grass-fed beef
ALAN AND MARY YEGERLEHNER
1087 East County Road 550 South
Clay City, IN 47841
812-939-2813
ayegerl@ccrtc.com

Traders Point Creamery
Organic yogurt, cheeses, ice cream, grass-fed beef
JANE ELDER KUNZ
9101 Moore Road
Zionsville, IN 46077
317-733-1700
www.tpforganics.com

Upland Brewing Company
Seasonal ales, stouts, and porters
350 West 11th Street
Bloomington, IN 47404
812-336-2337
www.uplandbeer.com

Wib's Stone Ground Grain
Cornmeal, grits, whole wheat flour, buckwheat flour
CHRIS VOSTER
812-636-8066 or 812-636-4622

Your Neighbor's Garden
Variety of Indiana fruits and vegetables
ROSS AND SHERRY FARIS
5224 Grandview Drive
Indianapolis, IN 46228
317-251-4130

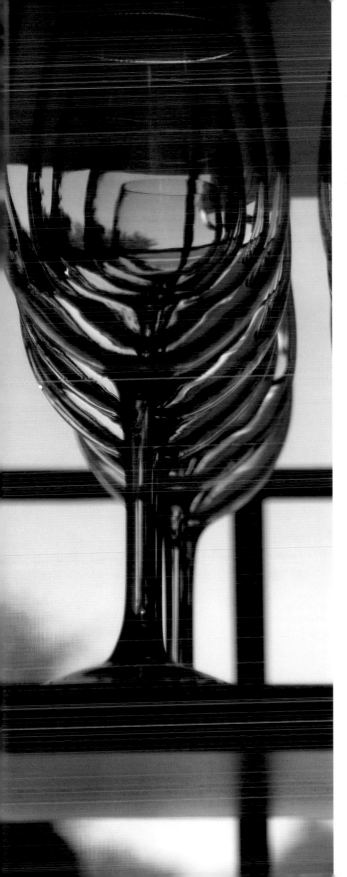

Recipe Index

RECIPES LISTED BY COURSE

RECIPES LISTED BY PRINCIPAL INGREDIENT(S)

Christine Barbour

teaches American politics and the politics of food at Indiana University, and writes a regular food column for the Bloomington *Herald-Times*. She is the co-author of two political science textbooks, and is currently writing a book on the fishing industry in Apalachicola, Florida. She is a founding member and co-leader of Slow Food Bloomington. Christine's website is www.christinebarbour.com.

Scott Feickert

is an administrator in the Political Science department at Indiana University. An avid home cook, he tested all the recipes in this book in his kitchen. He is also a founding member of Slow Food Bloomington.

Tom Stio

is a professional photographer living in Bloomington, Indiana. His specialties include portraiture and dance photography, and his fine art photographs have won numerous awards. Tom's website is www.kiva.net/~shadow.

Book and Jacket Designer	Sharon L. Sklar
Copy Editor	Dawn Ollila
Compositor	Sharon L. Sklar
Typeface	Minion
Book and Jacket Printer	Four Colour Imports